JESUS OF NAZARETH: A DELUDED MESSIAH

יֵשׁוּעַ הַנָּצְרִי מֶלֶךְ הַיְּהוּדִים

IESUS NAZARENUS REX IUDAEORUM

ʼIHΣOYS ʽO NAZΩPAIOS ʽO BAΣIΛEÝS TΩN ʼIOYΔAIΩN

JESUS THE NAZOREAN, KING OF THE JEWS – inscription placed on the cross of Jesus by Pontius Pilate (John 19: 19)

The 17th-century painting *Christ Crucified* by Diego Velázquez
(Museo del Prado in Madrid)

JESUS OF NAZARETH: A DELUDED MESSIAH

ALBERTUS PRETORIUS

WIPF & STOCK · Eugene, Oregon

JESUS OF NAZARETH
Jesus of Nazareth

Copyright © 2022 Albertus Pretorius. All rights reserved. Except for brief quotations in critical publications or reviews, no part of this book may be reproduced in any manner without prior written permission from the publisher. Write: Permissions, Wipf and Stock Publishers, 199 W. 8th Ave., Suite 3, Eugene, OR 97401.

Wipf & Stock
An Imprint of Wipf and Stock Publishers
199 W. 8th Ave., Suite 3
Eugene, OR 97401

www.wipfandstock.com

PAPERBACK ISBN: 978-1-6667-4664-8
HARDCOVER ISBN: 978-1-6667-4665-5
EBOOK ISBN: 978-1-6667-4666-2

CONTENTS

Chapter	Page
Foreword	xi
Introduction	1
1. The Conventional View of Jesus Christ in Christianity	5
2. What we do Know about Jesus	8
3. Jesus and his Contemporaries	27
4. The Arrest and Execution of Jesus	63
5. Jesus' Resurrection, Ascension, and Predictions	84
6. Views of the Original Christians Regarding Jesus	97
7. Paul's Visions and Revelations	122
8. Evaluation	144
Bibliography	153

List of Illustrations

Outside Cover: Jesus Christ, mosaic in the Hagia Sophia, Istanbul.
Frontispiece: The 17th-century painting *Christ Crucified* by Diego Velázquez, held by the Museo del Prado in Madrid
Solar eclipses: Downloaded from the NASA Eclipse Web Site
Lunar eclipses: Downloaded from the NASA Eclipse Website
Simulations of the night sky: Downloaded from a computerized recreation of the night sky by Stellarium
Chapter 4: Map of Ancient Jerusalem
IUDEA CAPTA coin
Chapter 5: Vespasian and Titus, the Roman generals and later emperors who vanquished the Jews during AD 66–70.
Chapter 7: Caravaggio: Conversion of St Paul (1601)

FOREWORD

This book is the result of a lifetime of study – theology, philosophy, history and psychology.

It is with a certain measure of trepidation and hesitation that this book is being presented to the world. I am very conscious of the fact that I am contradicting the beliefs of many people who hold firm religious views and whose faith is something dear to them. I have seen countless cases where a religious faith helped people to find meaning in life and to find guidance in the struggle between good and bad and right and wrong. Many people have found emotional and social support in their religious communities.

This book cannot but undermine those beliefs and I feel sorry for those people who might go through an intellectual and emotional struggle when they consider the evidence presented in this book.

However, it cannot be helped. I feel compelled to disclose the results of my investigations, ruminations, and own struggles and in the process unmask certain superstitions and even religious hypocrisy and fraud. If I don't do it, I won't be true to myself.

Albertus Pretorius, April 2022

INTRODUCTION

Jesus Christ, also known as Jesus of Nazareth, as well as Jesus the Nazorean, is arguably the most influential figure in the history of mankind. His followers, the adherents of Christianity, constitute the largest religious group in the world. More or less one third of all human beings call themselves Christians. Human history has been divided into the period before Christ (BC) and the period after Christ, usually expressed by die abbreviation AD (Anno Domini).

But – who was this Jesus of Nazareth or Jesus the Nazorean really?

An innumerable number of books have been written on this topic and it seems as if it is almost impossible to say anything new about this wandering preacher and healer of the first century who lived and died in the country of Palestine.

Yet, this is precisely what this book promises to do. The vast majority of the books written about Jesus take the information in the New Testament simply at face value. It is, though, necessary to investigate the texts of the gospels and other texts of the New Testament carefully and critically, without any overt religious or theological prejudice or ideology, yet also sympathetically – as any other historical text has to be studied to reconstruct the past, while keeping in mind the historical context in which they were compiled. Only this method makes it possible to come to a more realistic and reliable description of this remarkable man.

This approach was followed by various theologians and historians since the late eighteenth century in an effort to discover who and what Jesus of Nazareth really was, since they came to the conclusion that the information given in the New Testament amounts to religious propaganda and not an objective description of Jesus' life and ministry.

INTRODUCTION

Those authors who took part in the so-called Quest for the Historical Jesus, gave differing answers to the question: who and what was Jesus? They saw him respectively as a charismatic healer, a religious reformer, a revolutionary, an eschatological prophet, a learned teacher or rabbi, a cynic philosopher or an ascetic mystic. Although most of these may describe some aspects of Jesus' life and ministry, there was much more to this figure than only those characterizations.[1]

This book will endeavor to demonstrate that Jesus must, first of all, be seen as the king-in-waiting of the Jews. The following considerations will be argued at some length in the pages that follow:

- Jesus is often called the "Nazorean" in the gospels and Acts. It will be shown that that Jesus was regarded as a Nazarite, a person who dedicated his life to God and that he had close ties with the sect of the Essenes, who were also known as Nazoreans. The term "Nazorean" is usually erroneously translated as "Nazarene";
- Jesus called himself the "son of God" on various occasions. This title was applied exclusively to the kings of Israel in the Old Testament and Jesus, therefore, saw himself as the next king of Israel;
- The central theme of Jesus' message was the Kingdom of God/Heaven, which was to be established in the lifetime of his followers and of which he was to be the king. This was not a spiritual kingdom, but a political kingdom where the ancient kingdom of David was to be restored;

---

[1] Encyclopedia.com. "Historical Jesus".

INTRODUCTION

- Jesus often announced that he was only interested in liberating the "lost sheep of the house of Israel" – not people from other nations;
- Jesus was called the "son of David" on more than one occasion; that means that he was regarded as a descendant of King David, as well as his successor; and
- When Jesus was condemned to be crucified by the Roman governor, Pontius Pilate, the reason for the death sentence was precisely that he called himself the king of the Jews and behaved as such.

This book breaks new ground by coordinating the information given in the gospels and the rest of the New Testament with astronomical phenomena such as solar and lunar eclipses and the movements of the planets through the Zodiac. It will be shown that these phenomena played a hitherto neglected role in our knowledge about the life of Jesus, as well as dating certain events in the life of Jesus and providing a date for the compilation of the Gospel of Mark.

In addition, insights of neuroscience are taken into consideration. Ancient Jewish and Christian authors from the first to the fourth centuries AD will be quoted at appropriate places.

It will transpire that the dogmas created by Christian theologians and church councils about Jesus just cannot be sustained when all the available evidence is taken into account. This book will demonstrate that Jesus of Nazareth was nothing but a gifted man. He regarded himself as the king-in-waiting of the Jews and that he was the instrument chosen by the God of Israel to liberate his people from oppression by the Romans. He certainly was no divine figure who adopted a human body to become the savior of mankind. The only possible conclusion that can be made when all the evidence is carefully evaluated is that he was a tragically deluded messiah.

Of course, traditional Christians will brand this view as heretical. In previous centuries, views like this one would have

INTRODUCTION

resulted in the author burning on a stake in the town square with hundreds of hysterical Christians cheering and laughing at this sight. Fortunately, we live in an age where honest investigation is protected and people are free to believe whatever they want. It is to be expected that conservative religious authorities will condemn this book, but the possibility also exists that some of them will come to the point where they may accept that this book is making a valid point when they are presented with the evidence.

The traditional view of Jesus of Nazareth rests on the premise that the Bible, and especially the gospels, were inspired by the Holy Spirit and are, therefore, infallible. It will be shown, however, that this premise cannot be upheld. There are just too many contradictions, impossible tales and historical errors in the gospels for them to be regarded as divinely inspired. They have to be analyzed as any other ancient text has to be investigated – rationally, critically and sympathetically – while keeping the political, economic, judicial, and social circumstances of those times in mind.

CHAPTER 1
THE CONVENTIONAL VIEW OF JESUS CHRIST IN CHRISTIANITY

How is Jesus of Nazareth seen by most Christians? It is necessary to describe this conventional view briefly before an honest and thorough investigation of all available historical records can be undertaken to find out who Jesus of Nazareth really was.

In the Greek New Testament his name is Ἰησοῦς (*Iesous*). Most languages, including English, use the Latin transcription of this name, namely Jesus. His name in Hebrew or Aramaic – the home language of the Jews at the time – was *Yehoshua* (יְהוֹשֻׁעַ), which means: "Yahweh is salvation or deliverance," the same name of Joshua, the successor of Moses as leader of the Israelites.

The name – or rather title – of "Christ" means "anointed" and is derived from the Greek Χριστός (*Christos*). It is the Greek equivalent of the Hebrew מָשִׁיחַ (*mashiyach*), which is rendered in English as "messiah".

This Jesus is seen by most Christians as the divine Son of God, the second person in the divine trinity and the Christ (the anointed one or the Messiah) who became a human being in order to save sinners from the punishment they all deserve, namely eternal damnation and torture in hell.

The Creed of Nicaea, which was adopted by the Council of Nicaea (a town near Constantinople) in AD 325 and which was expanded in AD 381, is the oldest creed to state clearly that Jesus Christ had a dual nature – divine and human:

> "We believe.... in one Lord Jesus Christ, the only-begotten Son of God, begotten of the Father before all worlds, God of

1. THE CONVENTIONAL VIEW OF JESUS

God, Light of Light, Very God of Very God, begotten, not made, being of one substance with the Father by whom all things were made; who for us men, and for our salvation, came down from heaven, and was incarnate by the Holy Spirit of the Virgin Mary, and was made man, and was crucified also for us under Pontius Pilate. He suffered and was buried, and the third day he rose again according to the Scriptures, and ascended into heaven, and sitteth on the right hand of the Father. And he shall come again with glory to judge both the quick and the dead, whose kingdom shall have no end."

Other Christian creeds are essentially expansions of the formulation of Nicaea.

In other words: Jesus Christ is, according to orthodox Christianity, the second Person in the Trinity. He has a dual nature: divine and human. He was born from a virgin who was impregnated by the third Person in the Trinity, the Holy Spirit. As a human being, he was without sin. During his sojourn on earth, he ministered as a wandering teacher and healer. He was condemned to die on a cross as a common criminal by Pontius Pilate, the Roman governor of Judea. He was, though, resurrected on the third day, ascended to heaven and is expected to return on Judgment Day, sometime in the future. His death on the cross is seen as a vicarious atonement for the sins of all those who believe in him.

It has to be asked: is it possible to sustain this traditional view of Jesus when the available historical sources are scrutinized honestly and critically? In the pages that follow, it will be demonstrated that this view cannot any longer be defended if we take all known historical facts into consideration. There are more than enough indications in the New Testament, read together with other contemporary documents, that Jesus of Nazareth was an ordinary mortal human being. There can be no doubt that he was

1. THE CONVENTIONAL VIEW OF JESUS

extremely gifted and had a charismatic personality, but there was nothing divine or supernatural about him.

CHAPTER 2
WHAT WE DO KNOW ABOUT JESUS

The Gospels

Nobody with an open mind can doubt that Jesus of Nazareth was a real person and a historical figure. There are, though, those who dispute this. Timothy Freke and Peter Gandy, for instance, wrote two books, The Jesus Mysteries (1999) and Jesus and the Goddess (2002) to argue that Jesus was purely a mythical figure, modeled on the prototypes of the Egyptian god Osiris and the Greek god Dionysius. It has to be granted that there are some similarities between the depiction of Jesus in the Bible and pagan deities of the ancient world, but that does not mean that Jesus of Nazareth wasn't a historical personage. The view of Freke and Gandy is not supported by other historians and theologians.

There are a few snippets of information regarding Jesus in the work of Flavius Josephus, a Jewish historian of the first century AD, proving that he was a real human being. Some experts believe that one passage[2] (written around 93–94 AD) in which Jesus was described as a wise teacher who was executed by Pontius Pilate was inserted by a Christian scribe while copying the manuscript and that the paragraph in question was not part of the original manuscript. The passage in question reads as follows:

> "Now there was about this time Jesus, a wise man; if it be lawful to call him a man. For he was a doer of wonderful works; a teacher of such men as receive the truth with pleasure. He drew over to him both many of the Jews, and

---

[2] Flavius Josephus, *Antiquities of the Jews*, Book 18, III (3).

2. WHAT WE DO KNOW ABOUT JESUS

many of the Gentiles. He was [the] Christ. And when Pilate, at the suggestion of the principal men among us, had condemned him to the cross; those that loved him at the first did not forsake him. For he appeared to them alive again, the third day: as the divine prophets had foretold these and ten thousand other wonderful things concerning him. And the tribe of Christians, so named from him, are not extinct at this day."

Others believe an original (shorter) paragraph was augmented by a Christian scribe to add that Jesus was a messiah and more than a mere human being who was resurrected after his execution. If this passage of Josephus – or part of it – is genuine, then it only mentions the barest details, the most important being that Jesus, a wise teacher, had many followers and was executed by Pontius Pilate.[3]

Elsewhere, Josephus mentions "the brother of Jesus, who was called Christ, whose name was James", who was stoned in Jerusalem around AD 62[4] and experts agree that this passage is genuine. Josephus also refers to the death of another prominent figure in the New Testament, John the Baptist.[5] Most scholars regard this to be original as well.[6]

The Roman authors Tacitus, Pliny the younger and Suetonius from the end of the first century and the early second century AD mentioned that they knew of a new religious movement and that the adherents were called Christians. Nothing was said, though, about Christ himself after whom this movement was called, apart from the fact that Tacitus mentioned that Christ was executed by Pontius Pilate.

---

[3] Fredriksen, *Jesus of Nazareth, King of the Jews*, 249.
[4] Flavius Josephus, *Antiquities of the Jews*, Book 20, IX (1).
[5] Flavius Josephus, *Antiquities of the Jews*, Book 18, V (2).
[6] Poole, "Josephus, Flavius".

2. WHAT WE DO KNOW ABOUT JESUS

Some scholars also regard a remark in the letter of the Syrian Mara bar Serapion to his son – written shortly after AD 73 – as referring to Jesus, although he is not mentioned by name. The author of this letter mentions occasions when people killed three wise teachers from their midst – Socrates, Pythagoras and "the wise king" of the Jews – which ended in disaster for all of them. These three wise men, though, continue to live on through their wisdom.[7]

It is possible that Serapion refers to the destruction of Jerusalem in the recent past during the war against the Romans as a divine punishment for the execution of Jesus. The time period between the death of Jesus and the destruction of Jerusalem is almost four decades and it takes some imagination to link these two events. However, according to Eusebius of Caesarea, the Christian historian of the fourth century AD, there were those who saw the destruction of Jerusalem as divine punishment for the stoning of James, die brother of Jesus and his successor as leader of the Jesus Movement.[8]

It is, therefore, also possible that Serapion had James in mind, and not Jesus, when he wrote about the "wise king" who was killed by the Jews. After all, Jesus was not killed by the Jews (as will be shown later on in this book), while James was stoned by the Jews on behest of the chief Priest, Ananus.

The amount of authentic information regarding the life of Jesus of Nazareth from ancient non-Christian extrabiblical sources is, therefore, extremely meagre. The main sources of our knowledge of Jesus are, therefore, the four gospels contained in the New Testament.

The oldest parts of the New Testament, the epistles of Paul – written during the fifties and early sixties AD – contain very little biographical information about Jesus. We are only informed that

---

[7] Letter of Mara, Son of Serapion
[8] Eusebius, *Church History,* Liber II Chapter 23.

2. WHAT WE DO KNOW ABOUT JESUS

Jesus, the Son of God, was born of a woman, had king David of Israel as an ancestor, had a brother called James, had apostles called Cephas or Peter and John, instituted the Eucharist, was betrayed, was condemned to die on a cross, was resurrected and ascended to heaven, from where he is expected to return on Judgment Day.

Paul often makes allusions to the teachings of Jesus, including his teachings on marriage, his institution of the Eucharist and the resurrection of the dead on Judgment Day. One can assume that Paul did not find it necessary to contain many details regarding Jesus' life in his letters since he must have assumed that his readers were adequately informed. He reminded the recipients of his letter to the Galatians (3: 1) that to them "Jesus Christ has been vividly portrayed as on the Cross". In other words: he had told them the whole story of Jesus' execution as he knew it.

We don't know how well Paul was informed about the ministry of Jesus. He must have had some knowledge, due to his contact with the apostles and other Jewish followers of Jesus.

If we want to know more about Jesus, we have to rely on the four New Testament gospels, namely Matthew, Mark, Luke and John. The first three are known as the Synoptic Gospels since they relate essentially the same tale. John's Gospel contains much material not contained in the first three gospels.

There are also a number of noncanonical or apocryphal gospels from the second century AD, but the material contained in these writings does not seem to be very reliable.[9] The most reliable amongst them seems to be the Gospel of Thomas, which merely contains a number of sayings of Jesus, some of which also appear in the canonical gospels.[10]

---

[9] Pelikan, "Jesus Christ".
[10] Rylaardsdam et al., "Biblical literature".

2. WHAT WE DO KNOW ABOUT JESUS

We know next to nothing about Jesus' youth, his education and training or whether he was married and had children. We are informed, though, that he had brothers and sisters (Mark 6: 3; John 7: 5; Acts 1: 14). The gospels contain details of his teachings, his miracles, his trial, death and resurrection.

In Mark 6: 3 he is called a "carpenter" and in Matt 13: 55 he is mentioned as "the carpenter's son". The Greek word translated with "carpenter" is τέκτων (*tekton*). It may be translated as "carpenter", but may also mean "craftsman", "builder" and even "building contractor".

Since Jesus was evidently a learned man who knew the Hebrew Scriptures well, it may well be that he received a good education befitting the son of a well-to-do building contractor. Luke informs us that he was able to read, which not many people in those days were able to do (Luke 4: 17).

As a youngster, he reportedly attracted the attention of a number of teachers of the Law at the temple with his knowledge of and insight in the Hebrew Scriptures (Luke 2: 46–47). People regarded him as a learned man since he was often addressed as "Rabbi" – the title used for a Jewish teacher of the Law (Mark 9: 5; Mark 11: 21; Matt 26: 25, 49; John 1: 49; John 3: 2; John 9: 2 *etcetera*).

It is even possible that he knew some Greek,[11] which may explain why he was able to converse with the Roman governor, Pontius Pilate, during his trial.

As a learned Jewish rabbi, he must have regarded the Scriptures as reliable guides regarding matters of faith. His whole worldview was based on the Old Testament and his life was guided by the Law of Moses and the writings of the prophets.

---

[11] Fredriksen, *Jesus of Nazareth*, 162–64.

2. WHAT WE DO KNOW ABOUT JESUS

His teachings never amounted to a contradiction or rejection of these Scriptures, although he sometimes gave a novel and original interpretation thereof. There are no indications that he was influenced by Greek philosophy or any pagan religion. It can be safely said that he was a Jewish nationalist.

His ancestry from King David ought also to have played a role to place him and his family amongst the Jewish gentry. He and his family must have been well-known because the crowds in Jerusalem greeted him more than once with the words: "Hosanna to the son of David!" (Matt 21: 9, 15; see also Mark 11: 9–10).

The Authors of the Gospels
We do not really know who the authors of the gospels were and exactly where and when these documents were written, although their authorship was traditionally ascribed to certain apostles or other early Christians. What is clear, though, is that they all must have been compiled after the fall of Jerusalem and the destruction of the temple in AD 70 during the Jewish war against the Romans. All four contain a strong anti-Semitic flavor, in contrast to the epistles of Paul who wrote during the fifties and early sixties of the first century AD and who was proud of his Jewish ancestry and hoped that the Jews would accept Jesus as their Messiah (Gal 1:14; Phil 3: 5; Rom 11).

There are those who do not accept this dating of the gospels. Thiede and D'Ancona, for instance, tried to show that the Gospel of Matthew was written well before the seventies AD, based on two scraps of papyrus found in Egypt containing a few words, which seem to come from Matthew. They argue that the style of writing – the way the letters were formed and the abbreviations used – dates the document accurately to the sixties AD.[12] This is not very

---

[12] Thiede and D'Ancona, *The Jesus Papyrus,* 140

2. WHAT WE DO KNOW ABOUT JESUS

convincing because they also concede that a particular style of writing could reflect "the partial survival into the second century of much older stylistic traits".[13]

It will be shown later in this book that there is conclusive evidence in Mark 13 (especially Mark 13: 20, 24–25) that this gospel, the oldest gospel, was only written or finalized after AD 71.

The anti-Semitic attitude of the gospel writers becomes clear when one realizes that they pictured the Jews, especially the Pharisees, Sadducees, lawyers and priests, as plotting to get Jesus killed. Paul nowhere accuses the Jews of this crime. The Jews only became unpopular after the Jewish war of AD 66–70 during which Jerusalem with its temple was razed by the Roman army.

The gospels were not intended to give an objective description of the life and death of Jesus – they were works of propaganda in order to convince the Roman overlords of the time that Christianity was not to be confused with the Jewish religion, from which it departed and that it was an acceptable religion for sophisticated Greeks and Romans.[14]

The gospels and Acts are conspicuously silent about the hardship, cruelty, and poverty caused by the harsh Roman rule over Palestine during Jesus' lifetime – known from other sources. It will later be shown that the New Testament (with the exception of Revelation[15]) tried to picture the Romans as well disposed towards Jesus.

That the gospels are primarily propaganda is evident from the following introductory phrase in the Gospel of Mark: "The beginning of the gospel of Jesus Christ, the Son of God" (Mark 1: 1). The word "gospel" (Greek: εὐαγγέλιον – *euangelion*) has a specific meaning in this context, namely "good tidings". The book

---

[13] Thiede and D'Ancona, *The Jesus Papyrus,* 136.
[14] Cohn, *The Trial and Death of Jesus,* 246–47.
[15] Scholtz, *The Prophecies of Revelation.*

2. WHAT WE DO KNOW ABOUT JESUS

of Mark was, therefore, not written to give an objective account of the life and work of Jesus. It was rather written to convince people that it contained "good tidings" regarding Jesus, who is the Son of God (or a divine figure, such as many mythological figure of Antiquity). It was meant to convince people that it was worthwhile to read this book and get to know the Christ, the Messiah.

Towards the end of his gospel, John wrote:

> "Therefore, Jesus did many other signs in the presence of his disciples, which are not written in this book; but these are written, that you may believe that Jesus is the Christ, the Son of God, and that believing you may have life in his name" (John 20: 30–31).

In other words, John wrote his gospel with the sole purpose of convincing people to believe in Jesus and to accept that he is the Christ or Messiah and the Son of God.

Magee came to the conclusion that "the gospels were not written as accurate records for the archives but purely to persuade people to believe. They were not written as historical documents but to recruit converts..."[16]

There are also abundant signs that John used his purported reports about Jesus' sermons and teachings to disseminate his own religious and philosophical ideas. There are clear signs that John was influenced by Greek philosophy, especially when he called Jesus Christ the "Word" in the first chapter of his gospel. He wrote:

> "In the beginning was the Word, and the Word was with God, and the Word was God. The same was in the beginning with God. All things were made through him. Without him was not anything made that has been made. In him was life,

---

[16] Magee, "Christianity Revealed", 39.

and the life was the light of men. The light shines in the darkness, and the darkness hasn't overcome it. (...) The Word became flesh, and lived among us. We saw his glory, such glory as of the only Son of the Father, full of grace and truth" (John 1: 1–5, 14).

Key words in this passage are "Word", "life" and "light". The term "Word" is a translation of the Greek λόγος (*logos*), which has a very rich meaning. A biblical dictionary provides this explanation:

> "In John, [this term] denotes the essential Word of God, Jesus Christ, the personal wisdom and power in union with God, his minister in creation and government of the universe, the cause of all the world's life both physical and ethical, which for the procurement of man's salvation put on human nature in the person of Jesus the Messiah, the second person in the Godhead, and shone forth conspicuously from His words and deeds. A Greek philosopher named Heraclitus first used the term Logos around 600 B.C. to designate the divine reason or plan which coordinates a changing universe. This word was well suited to John's purpose in John 1."[17]

The Greek word for "life" is ζωή (*zoe*). A biblical dictionary explains that it refers to "the absolute fulness of life, both essential and ethical, which belongs to God, and through him both to the hypostatic 'logos' and to Christ in whom the 'logos' put on human nature."[18]

John uses the Greek word for "light" (φῶς – *fos*) in a metaphorical sense and according to a biblical dictionary it must be understood as follows: "God is light because light has the extremely

---

[17] Strong's Complete Greek & Hebrew Lexicon, "Logos".
[18] Strong's Complete Greek & Hebrew Lexicon, "Life".

2. WHAT WE DO KNOW ABOUT JESUS

delicate, subtle, pure, brilliant quality." It is also a metaphor "of truth and its knowledge, together with the spiritual purity associated with it, that which is exposed to the view of all, openly, publicly [and of] reason, mind – the power of understanding esp. moral and spiritual truth."[19]

This analysis makes it clear that the author (or the final editor) of the Gospel of John was influenced by Greek philosophy. His rendering of Jesus' sermons must be understood against this background. He applied the method used by many ancient historians of inventing a speech by a historical figure to fit the occasion. We must conclude that the reports of Jesus' teachings in the Gospel of John are for the most part the compositions of John (or the final editor) – and not the words of Jesus himself.

In other words: the Jesus in the Gospel of John is not a real person of flesh and blood but rather the embodiment or personification of certain Greek philosophical concepts.

The Bible contains many inconsistencies and historical errors, as well as impossible and improbable anecdotes. This is also true of the four gospels. They often contradict each other. As writings putting forth propaganda, it cannot be expected of them to contain an objective and factual description of the life of Jesus. It is, therefore, not possible to get an accurate picture of Jesus, what he did and taught and how he was condemned to die on a cross when one reads the gospels uncritically.

What we read about Jesus in the gospels is, therefore, always subject to correction. We have to take the political, economic, cultural, judicial, social and religious circumstances of his time into account. We must keep in mind that the gospel writers judged the circumstances under which Jesus lived from the perspectives of their own time, at least four decades after his death, when the scene had

---

[19] Strong's Complete Greek & Hebrew Lexicon, "Light".

2. WHAT WE DO KNOW ABOUT JESUS

changed dramatically after the fall of Jerusalem in AD 70. Their attitudes regarding the Roman authorities and the Jews were colored by their experiences during and after the Jewish war and they projected these attitudes upon the time when Jesus was alive, some decades earlier.

We must also consider that the writers of the Gospels were dependent upon oral and written traditions regarding the life and work of Jesus, as Luke reminds us in Luke 1: 1–4. Jesus left no writings and nobody wrote down what he did or said while he was still alive. The authors of the gospels were, therefore, dependent upon the memories of people who were eye witnesses and who passed their memories on to other people who joined the early Jesus Movement. As time passed, these memories got blurred and distorted and when they were eventually written down, decades after the events, they were colored and interpreted in the light of subsequent situations. Much of the information regarding Jesus as contained in the gospels is, therefore, legendary and even mythical in nature.

Magee's description of the origin and growth of the gospels is certainly correct:

> "The gospels have obviously been changed frequently by deliberating editing or by copying errors since they were first written, and it is not even clear that the gospels of Mark and Luke even existed in an agreed form at first. There is good reason for thinking that both could have existed initially as a draft form (proto-Mark and proto-Luke) and this was worked up by many hands into the books we now have. A similar scheme applies too to Matthew which was originally not at all like the gospel we now have but was a collection of sayings, perhaps a version of the document called "Q." This was combined with Mark, to give a fuller, richer and more

2. WHAT WE DO KNOW ABOUT JESUS

polished gospel and this was edited by many editors before it reached the modern form."[20]

That Magee is correct, is attested by the fact that there are, for instance, three different endings to the Gospel of Mark known to us. Luke reminds us at the beginning of his gospel (1: 1) that "many have undertaken to draw up a narrative concerning those matters" concerning the life and work of Jesus before he undertook this task. The report in John 8: 1–11 regarding the woman caught in adultery does not appear in the oldest manuscripts of this gospel and was only added at a later stage. There are clear indications that the last chapter in John, chapter 21, is an afterthought that was added later.

It also has to be remembered that the gospels were written in Greek, while Jesus and the Jews of his time spoke Aramaic. Transmitting the words of Jesus from Aramaic into Greek could have distorted his ideas and intentions. Since we will never know what Jesus said in Aramaic – with a few exceptions – it is not possible to gauge how accurately the authors of the gospels reported his teachings in Greek.[21]

The authors and editors of the gospels did not report how they gathered their information and assembled it into a coherent tale. Their method was likely to interview people who witnessed or remembered what Jesus said and did and to write their words down. Since none of these witnesses could provide a complete chronology of Jesus' ministry, the authors of Q (the oldest source about Jesus' teachings – see below) and Mark had to arrange their notes into some order with the object of constructing a credible and coherent gospel. Matthew and Luke merged Q with Mark, but added some material of their own. They also often rearranged Mark's

---

[20] Magee, "Christianity Revealed", 38.
[21] Fredriksen, *Jesus of Nazareth*, 162.

2. WHAT WE DO KNOW ABOUT JESUS

chronology. John contains a chronology that differs greatly from the other three gospels.

The material that the authors gathered long after the death of Jesus was not only interpreted by the authors of the gospels. We may assume that their informants also provided interpretations of their memories or the tales they heard from others in order to fit their information into the theological or religious scheme prevalent at that time.

It has to be stressed that especially Matthew often referred to certain passages in the Old Testament to "prove" that what Jesus experienced, said and did was the fulfillment of those prophecies. We may assume that he invented certain events in the belief that they must have happened since they were "predicted" in the Old Testament – although these "predictions" never really had Jesus in mind when they were written.

For instance: Matthew believed that Jer 31: 15 foretold that king Herod the Great would have all boys below two years of age in Bethlehem killed (Matt 2: 16–18). No independent record of this campaign of slaughter exists and it is most probably a piece of fiction. Nevertheless, in Jer 31: 15 we read the following (and it is quoted by Matthew as proof for his story):

> "A voice is heard in Ramah, lamentation, and bitter weeping, Rachel weeping for her children; she refuses to be comforted for her children, because they are no more."

When one reads the whole chapter in Jeremiah, it is clear that he referred to the laments that occurred after the Babylonians had sacked Jerusalem in 586 BC. Jeremiah never intended his words to be applied to the time of Herod the Great, centuries later.

It seems, on the other hand, that much reliable information was, indeed, included in the gospels.

2. WHAT WE DO KNOW ABOUT JESUS

The Gospel of John, for instance, contains the claim that it was authored by "the disciple who testifies about these things, and wrote these things. We know that his witness is true " (John 21: 24). On the other hand, this gospel was clearly edited at a later stage when certain parts were added – most probably the various philosophical discourses, which were clearly influenced by Greek philosophy. Bowman is of the opinion that the core of John, containing the more factual reports about Jesus' ministry, were written before the start of Jewish War against the Roman in AD 66, while the Jerusalem temple was still standing.[22]

Stendahl and Sander propose that "a working hypothesis is that John and the Johannine letters were written and edited somewhere in the East (perhaps Ephesus) as the product of a 'school,' or Johannine circle, at the end of the 1st century."[23] In other words, the gospel only got its final form at a fairly late date, although certain parts were written much earlier.

When one keeps in mind that the authors of the gospels and their informants tended to interpret the words and deeds of Jesus from the background of their own times, and one also strips the legendary, mythical, impossible and improbable elements away, one can often determine more or less what Jesus actually must have said, did and experienced. This may be especially the case when they reported something that seemingly did not quite fit their religious sentiments. One may assume in those cases that they, nevertheless, wrote down what they heard from their informants, although they did quite know what to make of it.

There are some experts on the New Testament, of which the so-called Jesus Seminar is the best known, who regard almost everything in the gospels to be fictitious or legendary. This book does not go so far. Although it will be shown that there are various

---

[22] Bowman, "Historical Jesus", 15–18; see also Hendricks, "The Gospel According to John", 147.
[23] Stendahl and Sander, "Biblical Literature".

2. WHAT WE DO KNOW ABOUT JESUS

inconsistencies, improbabilities and impossibilities contained in the gospels, there is also much that preserved authentic memories, although these memories often got skewed during the decades separating the life of Jesus and the eventual recording of them a few decades later.

Inconsistencies and Contradictions
That the stories regarding Jesus contained in the gospels cannot always be trusted is, for instance, evident from the fact that the two gospels containing nativity stories, Matthew and Luke, contradict each other almost totally.

For a start: both of them provided their readers with a genealogy of Jesus to show how he descended from the Israelite King David (Matt 1: 1–17 and Luke 3: 23–38). It is not possible to reconcile these genealogies since they contain, for the most part, different names. At least one of them must, therefore, be an invention. It has to be pointed out that both these genealogies present Joseph as Jesus' father, while both Matthew and Luke also emphasize that Jesus' mother was still a virgin when he was born – which means that Joseph could not have been his father.

According to Matthew, an angel appeared to Joseph, the betrothed of Mary, to inform him that his virgin bride was pregnant from the Holy Spirit and that he should not break off the engagement. A passage from Isaiah was quoted to explain this virgin birth. Jesus was born in specifically Bethlehem as the fulfillment of another prophecy of the Old Testament. Star gazers or astrologers from the east visited the baby Jesus in Bethlehem. When King Herod heard that a new king was born, he ordered that all boys below the age of two in Bethlehem be killed. Joseph was, though, warned again by an angel to escape to Egypt where he and his family stayed until Herod had died.

2. WHAT WE DO KNOW ABOUT JESUS

There are various improbable and impossible elements in this tale. First of all, it was not necessary to flee to Egypt to save the baby Jesus. Joseph resided in Nazareth, a village in Galilee in the north of Palestine (Matt 2: 23; Luke 2: 39–51) and he could simply have returned home to escape Herod's killing bands that concentrated their efforts on Bethlehem, which lies south of Jerusalem.

The quotation from Isaiah rests on a misunderstanding. Isaiah mentioned in chapter 7: 14 of his book that a certain unnamed young women of his time – not a virgin – would become pregnant. The Greek translation of the Old Testament made a mistake by altering "young woman" or "maiden" to "virgin". This passage in Isaiah can, therefore, in no way be seen as a prediction that Jesus would be born from a virgin.

Luke, on the other hand, tells his readers that the Virgin Mary was visited by an angel who announced that she would become pregnant through the Holy Spirit and that her son would become a great king, just as his ancestor David. The angel reportedly said: "The Lord God will give to him the throne of his father, David" (Luke 1: 32).

She and her fiancé, Joseph, had to go to Bethlehem, Joseph's ancestral home town, for a population census during the time when Quirinius was governor of Syria. There Jesus was born and he was visited by some shepherds who heard of the birth of the savior of Israel from a choir of angels. After this, the baby Jesus was taken to the temple in Jerusalem by his parents to be dedicated to God. Two aged prophets, Simeon and Anna, found the family at the temple and blessed the baby. Finally, the family moved back to Nazareth, Joseph's home town.

Luke's tale coincides with Matthew's version only in two respects, namely that Jesus' mother was a virgin who was impregnated by the Holy Spirit and that he was born in Bethlehem.

2. WHAT WE DO KNOW ABOUT JESUS

Luke seems unaware of the visit of the astrologers from the East, Herod's killing of the children in Bethlehem or the flight to Egypt. Matthew, likewise, knew nothing of the census, the shepherds, the visit to the temple and the immediate return to Nazareth. Both tales contain different supernatural heavenly beings who conveyed messages, which put them in the realm of myths.

Jesus must have been born before Herod's death in 2 BC, at the time when a census in the time of P. Sulpicius Quirinius, governor of Syria, took place as ordered by Emperor Tiberius (Luke 2: 1–2).[24] Luke's explanation for the visit to Bethlehem, where the baby was born, however, does not make sense. The object of a census was always to count the population at their place of residence – not at the home of an ancestor who lived centuries earlier – in order to draw up a budget for taxation purposes. An encyclopedia explains: "Every five years, the Romans enumerated citizens and their property to determine their liabilities."[25]

Both nativity stories in Matthew and Luke suggest that Jesus was born out of wedlock since Joseph was only engaged to Mary when Jesus was born. If that really was the case, then that might be the reason why the couple went to Bethlehem for the delivery and didn't stay in their home village, Nazareth, in order to spare Mary the condemnation of the villagers.

On the other hand, the fact that Jesus became a popular teacher and that the crowds greeted him as their king when he entered JeruSalem on the back of an ass a few days before his execution, suggest that he could not have been born out of wedlock and that his parents must have been legally married. After all, we read in Deut 23: 2 –

---

[24] Gertoux, "Herod the Great and Jesus", 28,
[25] Encyclopaedia Britannica, "Census".

2. WHAT WE DO KNOW ABOUT JESUS

> "One whose father and mother are not married may not come into the meeting of the Lord's people, or any of his family to the tenth generation."

If Jesus was really born out of wedlock, he would have been treated as a social outcast, a pariah. Instead, he was regarded as a charismatic preacher, an authoritative teacher and a gifted healer who drew large crowds. They repeatedly hailed him as the son of David and a pretender to the throne of Israel (Matt 1: 1; Matt 9: 27; Matt 21: 9; Matt 22: 42; Mark 11: 10; Luke 1: 32; John 7: 42). The reason for his execution was precisely that he thought of himself as the king-in-waiting of the Jews and a notice to that effect was placed on his cross. Therefore, his parents must have been legally married when he was born. Only one conclusion can be reached: both nativity tales in Matthew and Luke do not record real events. They were invented to provide "proof" that Jesus was *the* Messiah who had been promised by the prophets of the Old Testament.

In other words: we have possibly only the word of Mary and Joseph that Jesus was born of a virgin. There are no independent witnesses for this allegation and it cannot be verified at all. But on the other hand, these nativity stories most probably did not come from Mary and Joseph but were the inventions of Matthew and Luke for the sake of propaganda in support of the early Christian movement.

There are the following examples of mythological virgin births in Antiquity and it is clear that Jesus' purported virgin birth was modelled on these examples:

- The Egyptian god Horus was born from a virgin, Isis. He was visited after his birth by wise men;
- The Greek god Adonis was born of the virgin Myrrha;
- Perseus, the Greek god, also had a virgin for a mother;

2. WHAT WE DO KNOW ABOUT JESUS

- Herakles (Hercules), the Greek hero and demi-god, had the king of the gods, Zeus, and a virgin mother as parents;
- The Persian god, Mithras, was born of a virgin; he was later venerated by many Roman soldiers;
- The Persian prophet, Zoroaster, also had a virgin for a mother;
- The mother of the Greek philosopher Plato was reputedly impregnated by Apollo before she and her husband could have had intercourse;
- The Greek conqueror, Alexander the Great, was born after his mother was reputedly impregnated by either a divine snake or a thunderbolt, sent by Zeus;
- The legendary founders of the city of Rome, Romulus and Remus, were born from a vestal virgin, Rhea Sylvia, and their father was the war god Mars; and
- The first Roman emperor, Augustus, claimed that he was sired by the sun god, Apollo.[26]

With the meager knowledge of medical science in antiquity and the belief in magic and miracles, the idea of Jesus' virgin birth would have been very acceptable to the original readers of the gospels. They would actually have expected the Messiah and a divine figure like Jesus to have been born in exceptional circumstances. It turned out, in the meantime, that it is just not possible for a woman to become pregnant without the semen of a man, which is usually delivered through sexual intercourse.

It may be pointed out that the holy book of Islam, the Qur'an (Sura 19), repeats the tradition of the virgin birth of Jesus, although his divinity is denied.

---

[26] Ontario Consultants on Religious Tolerance, "The Virgin Birth (Conception) of Jesus"; Hitchens, *God is not Great*, 23; Wolmarans, "Jesus", 196–224.

CHAPTER 3
JESUS AND HIS CONTEMPORARIES

Before the tragic death of Jesus can be discussed, it is, first of all, necessary to introduce the main role players in this drama: the Romans, the various Jewish religious and political movements and Jesus himself:

The Roman Empire and Pontius Pilate
After the death of the Greek conqueror Alexander the Great, his empire was divided by his generals. Palestine eventually ended up under the reign of the Seleucids, the kings of Syria. A successful revolt under the leadership of the Maccabees during the second century BC led to the establishment of an independent Jewish kingdom. Strife between opposing factions that supported different pretenders to the throne led John Hyrcanus II to appeal to Rome for help. Pompey, a Roman general, intervened and Judea came under Roman control in 63 BC.

The country was initially ruled by client kings of which the most well-known was Herod the Great (ruled 37–2 BC). After his death and the removal of his son and heir who proved to be incompetent, a Roman governor was appointed to administer Judea.[27]

Pontius Pilate was appointed governor or prefect of Judea by Emperor Tiberius in AD 26, during Jesus' lifetime. The depiction of his character as being weak and easily swayed by the Jewish leadership in the four gospels does not tally with a more impartial

---

[27] Rylaarsdam et al., "Biblical Literature".

assessment by Flavius Josephus, the ancient Jewish historian. According to him, Pilate was proud, headstrong, cruel and resolute. He harbored no love for the Jews and showed gross disrespect for their religion on more than one occasion. His task was to uphold Roman law in this far-flung province, to quell any sign of rebellion and to punish those who were found guilty of *crimen maiestatis* – an insult to the emperor or his representative, the governor – by crucifixion.[28]

It is also necessary to provide a brief description of the main religious and political groups at the time when Jesus lived: The Sadducees, the Pharisees and the Essenes.

The High Priest, the Sanhedrin, and the Sadducees

In Roman times, the high priesthood in Jerusalem was confined to a few families who belonged to the party of the liberal and aristocratic Sadducees and who could pay for the privilege. When Jesus was tried, the high priest was Caiaphas, son-in-law of Annas, the retired former high priest.[29]

The high priest presided over the Sanhedrin, the Jewish council, which had jurisdiction over internal Jewish political and religious matters. There were 71 members of which the majority belonged to the party of the Pharisees, a group of conservative Jews (see below). The council was comprised of priests, Levites, lay aristocrats and scholars or teachers of the Law.[30]

The high priest was responsible to the Roman governor who appointed him and his task was to keep law and order and to prevent any form of rebellion. He also needed the support of the Sanhedrin

---

[28] Flavius Josephus: War, Liber II/IX/2-4; Cohn, *The Trial and Death of Jesus*, 14–15; Encyclopaedia Britannica, "Pontius Pilate".

[29] Cohn, *The Trial and Death of Jesus*, 22–24.

[30] Cohn, *The Trial and Death of Jesus*, 24–26.

3. JESUS AND HIS CONTEMPORARIES

to execute his duties and pursue his policies, which included the smooth running of the temple complex in Jerusalem. The Sanhedrin had the power to punish people when they were found guilty of transgressing the Law of Moses. The punishment for blasphemy was death by stoning (Lev 24: 16).[31] It may be assumed that Caiaphas and the members of the council tried their best to further Jewish interests, within the constraints placed upon them by the Roman occupation of Judea.[32]

The party of the Sadducees, which is often mentioned in the gospels, usually cooperated with the Roman authorities.[33]

The Pharisees

The authors of the gospels did not seem to be sure about the attitude of the Pharisees, the members of a conservative religious movement that tried to live according to the Law of Moses, towards Jesus. On the one hand, they were described as Jesus' opponents:

- "The Pharisees went out, and immediately took counsel with the Herodians against him [Jesus], how they might destroy him' (Mark 3:6).
- "But the Pharisees went out, and took counsel against him [Jesus], how they might destroy him" (Matt 12: 14).

These words suggest that the Pharisees were Jesus' enemies who wanted to get rid of him. The following passage from Luke 13: 31, on the other hand, tells a different story:

---

[31] Cohn, *The Trial and Death of Jesus*, 30–31.
[32] Cohn, *The Trial and Death of Jesus*, 27.
[33] Rylaardsdam *et.al.* "Biblical Literature."

3. JESUS AND HIS CONTEMPORARIES

"On that same day, some Pharisees came, saying to him [Jesus], 'Get out of here, and go away, for Herod wants to kill you.'"

If the Pharisees really were hostile towards Jesus, they would never have warned him to remove himself from mortal danger. What we know of the Pharisees suggests that they must have been sympathetic towards Jesus since their religious views coincided in more than one respect.[34] Two prominent members of the party of the Pharisees, Nicodemus and Joseph of Arimathea, were known supporters of Jesus and they buried him after his death (John 3; John 19: 38–39).

A leader of the Pharisees and member of the Sanhedrin, Gamaliel, showed his sympathy with the followers of Jesus when they were tried by the Sanhedrin for purportedly teaching a false doctrine (Acts 5: 38–39). We are informed in Acts 15: 5 that a number of Pharisees believed in Jesus and joined the followers of Jesus in Jerusalem after his crucifixion, which would not have happened if the Pharisees really thought that Jesus was a blasphemer or a heretic.

It must be concluded that the Pharisees were pictured in the gospels as Jesus' enemies in order to vilify the Jews and to exonerate the role of the Roman authorities in Jesus' execution. The truth is, though, that most Pharisees were actually well disposed towards Jesus.

The Essenes
The Jewish party or sect of the Essenes was a semi-ascetic group that practiced celibacy in some instances. In cases where their members did get married, they regarded these unions as unbreakable

---

[34] Cohn, *The Trial and Death of Jesus*, 66.

3. JESUS AND HIS CONTEMPORARIES

and divorce was forbidden. A number of them were priests who regarded the Jerusalem priesthood of the party of the Sadducees as corrupt and false due to their cooperation with the Roman overlords. Some of them may be described as Nazarites due to their sober and ascetic lifestyle and, according to their own literature, they followed the strict rules imposed upon Nazarites in Num 6. They had strong Messianic expectations and awaited royal and priestly messiahs.[35]

Various researchers are of the opinion that John the Baptist had links with this sect, due to his lifestyle and message.[36]

The name "Essenes" (Greek: Ἐσσηνοί, Ἐσσαῖοι, or Ὀσσαῖοι – *Essenoi, Essaioi* or *Ossaioi*) does not occur in the New Testament and many scholars thought that the authors of the gospels simply ignored them and that our knowledge about them is only to be found in the writings of Flavius Josephus, Pliny the Elder, Philo of Alexandria and other ancient authors.[37]

However, they do appear repeatedly under another name in the New Testament, namely that of the "Nazoreans" (Ναζωραῖοι – *Nazoraioi*).

According to Epiphanios, the bishop of Constantia on Cyprus, who wrote a lengthy book, the Panarion, during the last half of the fourth century AD in which he criticized all the heresies of his time, the sect of the Essenes, which he called the Ὀσσαῖοι, Ὀσσηνοι or Ἰεσσαῖοι (*Ossaioi, Ossenoi* or *Jessaioi*), was none other than the Nazoreans.[38]

---

[35] Encyclopaedia Britannica, "Essenes"; Rylaarsdam et al., "Biblical Literature".

[36] Pixner, "Jerusalem's Essene Gateway"; Strugnell, "John the Baptist"; see also: Epiphanios, *Panarion,* Liber I, 19:1–6

[37] Duling, "The Jewish World"; Encyclopaedia Britannica, "Essenes".

[38] Epiphanios, *Panarion,* Liber I, 19:1–6, 29: 1–5.

3. JESUS AND HIS CONTEMPORARIES

Other modern scholars concur with him.[39]

Jesus is often called a Nazorean in the gospels and Acts (Matt 2: 23; Matt 26:71; Luke 18:37, John 18:5, 7; John 19: 19; Acts 2: 22; Acts 3: 6, Acts 4: 10; Acts 6: 14, Acts 22: 8; and Acts 26: 9). In other words: Jesus was a member of the sect of the Essenes or was closely associated with them.

The Greek name of "Nazorean" is probably derived from the Hebrew word "branch" as used in Isaiah and Daniel, namely נֵצֶר (netzer).[40] After all, according to the dictionaries consulted, the word "Nazorean" means "one separated or a Nazarite".

Kinzig notes: "In ancient rabbinical literature, too, the Christians are occasionally referred to as נוצרים (nosrim)"[41] – which seems to confirm the connection of the name "Nazorean" with the Hebrew word נֵצֶר (netzer).

In addition, the Greek word for "Nazorean" (Ναζωραῖος – Nazoraios) may also have a connection with the Hebrew word for Nazarite, namely נָזִיר (Nazir), which means "a consecrated or devoted one."

In Matt 2: 23, we read that there was a prophecy that Jesus would be a Nazorean "that it might be fulfilled which was spoken through the prophets: 'He will be called a Nazorean.'"

This prophecy was most probably to be found in Isa 11: 1 where it is said of the Messiah: "There shall come forth a shoot out of the stock of Jesse, and a branch out of his roots shall bear fruit."

Isaiah 62: 21 is another prophecy that may have been meant: "Your people also shall be all righteous; they shall inherit the land

---

[39] International Standard Bible Encyclopedia Online, "Essenes", and the McClintock and Strong Biblical Encyclopedia, "Jessaeans".
[40] Duling, "The Jewish World"; Kinzig, "The Nazoreans", 470.
[41] Kinzig, "The Nazoreans", 471

3. JESUS AND HIS CONTEMPORARIES

forever, the branch of my planting, the work of my hands, that I may be glorified" (see also: Dan 11: 7).

Jesus was also called a Nazorean on the inscription on his cross (John 19: 19). His followers after his death were, accordingly, called "the sect of the Nazoreans" (Acts 24: 5).

The name "Nazorean" should not be confused with the name of "Nazarene" – as happened in most translations of the Bible. Saint Jerome, the translator of the Bible into Latin, the Vulgate, made this mistake and he used the word "Nazarenus" every time he encountered the Greek word Ναζωραῖος (*Nazoraios*) – except for Matt 2: 23. His example was followed by most other translators.

However, the authoritative Greek–English dictionary of Arndt and Gingrich explains that Ναζωραῖος (*Nazoraios*) and Ναζαρηνός (*Nazarenos* – Nazarene) are two totally different and unrelated words and that there is no linguistic connection between them. The word "Nazarene" is used for people from the town of Nazareth where Jesus grew up. The name "Nazarene" was often used of Jesus and he was, accordingly, sometimes called "Jesus of Nazareth" or "Jesus the Nazarene" (Mark 1: 24; Mark 10: 47; Mark 14: 67; Mark 16: 6; Luke 4: 34; and Luke 24: 19).

The name "Nazorean", on the other hand, means "one separated [as a branch from the trunk, as the Essenes separated themselves from the other Jews] or a Nazarite". According to Josephus, the Essenes also kept themselves separate from other Jews while living in communities in various towns and villages where they shared all their belongings. Josephus adds:

> "These men are despisers of riches… (and) that those who come to them must let what they have be common to the whole order, insomuch that among them all there is no appearance of poverty, or excess of riches, but every one's possessions are intermingled with every other's possessions,

3. JESUS AND HIS CONTEMPORARIES

> and so there is, as it were, one patrimony among all the brethren. (. . .) They have no one certain city, but many of them dwell in every city; and if any of their sect come from other places, what they have lies open for them, just as if it were their own…"[42]

The aversion of the Nazoreans or Essenes against wealth and opulence stems from their antipathy against the rich and affluent Sadducees.

It is clear the Jesus' disciples and followers lived according to these principles. When Jesus sent his twelve disciples and later 72 of his followers to spread the news about the imminent establishment of the Kingdom of God, he ordered them not to take a purse with money along but to rely on the hospitality of those where they lodged (Luke 9: 3–5; 10: 1–3), just as the Essenes did when they travelled and lodged with other members of their sect. When the 72 reported back to Jesus, he asked them: "'When I sent you out without purse, and wallet, and shoes, did you lack anything?' They said, 'Nothing'" (Luke 22:35).

The fact that the two words, "Nazorean" and "Nazarene", are often regarded as synonyms results from Matt 2: 23 where the name of the town "Nazareth" and the name "Nazonean" occur in the same sentence. We read there that Joseph and his family "came and lived in a city called Nazareth; that it might be fulfilled which was spoken through the prophets: 'He will be called a Nazorean.'"

This does not mean that the author of Matthew thought that the name "Nazorean" was somehow derived from the name of the village of Nazareth. He must have known full well that the two words have nothing in common and he only made use of a play of words with two similar-sounding words in one sentence.

---

[42] Josephus. *Wars*, *II(8)*.

3. JESUS AND HIS CONTEMPORARIES

The best proof that the names "Nazarene" and "Nazorean" are not synonyms or two versions of the same word, is Acts 24: 5 where Paul is called "a ringleader of the sect of the Nazarenes", according to most translations. This translation doesn't make sense. The sect in question certainly didn't consist of people from Nazareth only – they came from Jerusalem and other parts of Judea and Galilee. Paul can by no stretch of imagination be called a "Nazarene", a native of Nazareth. It makes much more sense to regard this sect to be the "Nazoreans" – in other words, Essenes – as stated explicitly in the Greek text and which is usually given a wrong translation by transforming "Nazoreans" to "Nazarenes".

It has to be added that Epiphanios, who wrote his book to expose the heresies of various sects in the early church, made a clear distinction between the "Nazarenes" and the "Nazoreans".[43]

The headquarters of the Essenes or Nazoreans was at the monastery of Qumran on the shores of the Dead Sea. Scholars agree that the so-called Dead Sea Scrolls, found in nearby caves since 1947, were actually the library of this sect that was hidden in safe places during the Jewish revolt against the Romans in AD 66–70.[44]

Josephus mentioned that the Essenes lived in many towns and villages in Palestine, including Jerusalem.[45] Archaeologists have located the Essene Quarter in ancient Jerusalem of Jesus' time, namely in the south western corner of the walled city. There was a gate in the city wall next to this quarter, called by Josephus the "Gate of the Essenes". Directly outside this gate the ritual baths and

---

[43] Epiphanios, *Panarion,* Liber 1: 19, 29.
[44] Pixner, "Jerusalem's Essene Gateway"; Rylaarsdam et al. "Biblical Literature".
[45] Josephus, *Wars,* Liber II, 8: 119–161.

ablution facilities of these Essenes were to be found,[46] including the pool of Siloam, mentioned in John 9: 7, 11 (see the map).

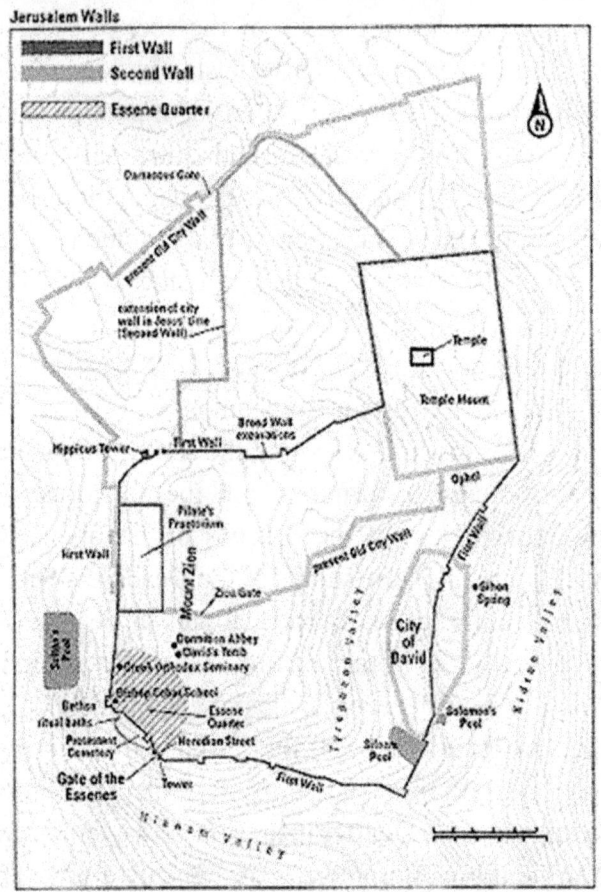

Map of Jerusalem before the destruction of the city by the Romans in AD 70. The Essene Quarter was in die south western corner (the shaded area), directly south of Pontius Pilate's Praetorium or Court House.

Jesus of Nazareth

Jesus was a popular Jewish teacher and a healer. Many people with psychosomatic ailments, probably due to the extreme stress they

---

[46] Pixner, "Jerusalem's Essene Gateway".

3. JESUS AND HIS CONTEMPORARIES

were subjected to on account of poverty and the harsh Roman rule, sought relief from Jesus. They often attributed these ailments to demonic possession since they had no other explanations for their conditions.[47]

There is the possibility that Jesus acquired some knowledge of medicine from the Essenes. Josephus wrote about this sect: "They also take great pains in studying the writings of the ancients, and choose out of them what is most for the advantage of their soul and body; and they inquire after such roots and medicinal stones as may cure their distempers."[48]

Although Jesus was later – according to the gospels – accused of blasphemy, there is, however, nothing in his words or actions as reported to justify such an accusation. He healed the sick, he told sinners that their sins were forgiven, he explained the Jewish Law (Torah) and he called God his Father. He declared that God would visit judgment upon the Jews due to their sinful ways. Of course, the Jews accused the Christians later on of spreading a false doctrine and the authors of the gospels projected this state of affairs onto the life of Jesus.

There was nothing in the Law to prohibit these actions and pronouncements and it is unthinkable that the Jewish authorities would have plotted to have him executed because of what he did and said – especially because he was such a popular figure with a large following. He followed the examples of the Old Testament prophets in many respects and the Sanhedrin must have respected that.[49]

The gospels often portray Jesus as condemning and cursing the Pharisees for being hypocrites – in contravention to his own

---

[47] Armstrong, *Fields of Blood*, 123.
[48] Josephus. *Wars*, II(8).
[49] Cohn, *The Trial and Death of Jesus*, 53–54.

3. JESUS AND HIS CONTEMPORARIES

dictum that one should love one's enemies.[50] That must be an exaggeration since certain Pharisees were well disposed towards him, as has been shown.

It has been said in the gospels that he alienated and angered the priestly class by his overturning the tables of money changers and sellers of sacrificial animals at the temple (Mark 11:15–18). Cohn argues that they would have actually applauded this action since it could not have taken place within the temple itself, but outside the temple building on the temple mount.[51] Fredriksen adds that the flocks of sacrificial animals could not have been kept in a temple courtyard since they would have fouled the precincts.[52]

Nobody needed a license from the temple management to put a stall up in those days and there seems to have been a number of dishonest businessmen, whose actions Jesus could not tolerate. There is no independent evidence that the priests profited from the sale of sacrificial animals or the exchange of foreign money for currency acceptable to the temple authorities. If Jesus did something unlawful or endangered the interests of the priestly class, they would have had him arrested immediately by the temple guards – which certainly did not happen. Instead, the temple authorities would rather have tolerated or even supported his actions.[53]

It may be added that Matthew reports that Jesus' action was applauded even by the children at the temple (Matt 21: 15). What he did must, therefore, have found favor with the ordinary Jews who attended the feast.

---

[50] Cohn, *The Trial and Death of Jesus*, 39.
[51] Cohn, *The Trial and Death of Jesus*, 54–59
[52] Fredriksen, *Jesus of Nazareth*, 232.
[53] Cohn, *The Trial and Death of Jesus*, 54–59; Fredriksen, *Jesus of Nazareth*, 232.

3. JESUS AND HIS CONTEMPORARIES

According to the gospels, Jesus predicted that he would be killed by the Jews:

- "For he taught his disciples, and said to them, 'The Son of Man is delivered up into the hands of men, and they will kill him; and when he is killed, on the third day he will rise again'" (Mark 9: 31).
- "Behold, we are going up to Jerusalem. The Son of Man will be delivered to the chief priests and the scribes. They will condemn him to death, and will deliver him to the Gentiles. They will mock him, spit on him, scourge him, and kill him. On the third day he will rise again" (Mark 10: 33–34).
- "The Son of Man must suffer many things, and be rejected by the elders, chief priests, and scribes, and be killed, and the third day be raised up" (Luke 9: 22).
- "From that time, Jesus began to show to his disciples that he must go to Jerusalem and suffer many things from the elders, chief priests, and scribes, and be killed, and the third day be raised up" (Matt 16: 21).

There can be little doubt that the gospel writers put these words in Jesus' mouth in order to prepare their readers for the subsequent narrative that it was the Jewish leaders – and not the Roman authorities ("the Gentiles") – who sought Jesus' death.[54]

Jesus' Marital State
It was always taken for granted that Jesus died a bachelor since the gospels don't mention a wife. However, Michael Baigent, Richard Leigh and Henry Lincoln caused quite a stir during the eighties of

---

[54] Cohn, *The Trial and Death of Jesus,* 64–65.

the previous century with their book The Holy Blood and the Holy Grail – a book that was reprinted many times.

Baigent *et al.* argued that Jesus was married to Mary Magdalene and that the wedding feast at Cana as described in John 2: 1–11, was actually his own wedding. They based their conclusion mainly on noncanonical gospels.[55] This idea was reworked into a best-selling novel by Dan Brown, the Da Vinci Code, and a film version with Tom Hanks in the main role. Dan Burstein edited a book, Secrets of the Code, in which it was shown that many scholars questioned the research methods and conclusions of Baigent *et al.*[56]

The silence of the gospels on Jesus' marital state can easily be explained. As an Essene or Nazorean, as well as a Nazarite, it would have been expected of him to stay celibate. He, however, held marriage in high regard as is evident from Mark 10: 9 where he declared: "What therefore God has joined together, let no man separate." With this, he actually differed from the Torah in which divorce was allowed (Mark 10: 1–8; Deut 24: 1–4) and he only reiterated the Essene point of view.

A King-in-Waiting
The Jews of Jesus' time – including the Essenes or Nazoreans, of which sect Jesus was a member or an associate – experienced great hardship under the rule of Herod the Great and the Roman governors and they longed for a savior to liberate them and restore the ancient kingdom of David. This yearning is perhaps best formulated in the Psalms of Solomon, a collection of hymns from the first century BC when Palestine came under Roman rule. Toy provides this summary of the contents of this hymn book:

---

[55] Baigent at al. *The Holy Blood,* 346 – 366.
[56] Burstein, *Secrets of the Code,* 177.

3. JESUS AND HIS CONTEMPORARIES

"The book consists of eighteen psalms, the contents of which may be summarized as follows: suffering inflicted by foreign invasion (i., viii.); desecration of Jerusalem and the temple, death in Egypt of the invader (ii.); debauchery of Jewish 'men-pleasers' (iv.); recognition of God's justice in rewarding the pious and in punishing the wicked (iii., vi., ix., x., xiii., xiv., xv.); expectation of and prayer for divine intervention (vii., xi., xii., xvi.); description of the Messiah (xvii., xviii.)."[57]

The need for a messiah is perhaps best expressed in Ps 17 of this collection:

23. "Behold, oh Lord, and raise up unto them their king, the son of David, At the time the which Thou seest, o God, that he may reign over Israel thy servant
24. And gird him with strength, that he may shatter unrighteous rulers,
25. And that he may purge Jerusalem from nations that trample (her) down to destruction. wisely, righteously.
26. He shall thrust out sinners from (the) inheritance, He shall destroy the pride of the sinner as a potter's vessel. With a rod of iron, he shall break in pieces all their substance, He shall destroy the godless nations with the word of his mouth."[58]

It has already been mentioned that the gospels and Acts are totally silent regarding the harshness, cruelty and inhumanity of the Roman rule. These works were only composed after the Romans had destroyed Jerusalem with its temple to end the Jewish revolt of AD 66–70. No author of a gospel could have dared to criticize the

---

[57] Toy, "The Psalms of Solomon".
[58] Gray, "The Psalms of Solomon", 631–52.

3. JESUS AND HIS CONTEMPORARIES

Romans in those circumstances. All the blame for Jesus' execution was, therefore, placed upon the unpopular Jews. However, there was an urgent need for a messiah, a savior, somebody to deliver the Jews from the horrible Roman yoke.

Although the Old Testament mentions several messiahs, people anointed on behalf of God, such as kings, prophets, and priests, there was a strong expectation on account of several prophecies that a descendant of King David would take up the throne in Jerusalem and establish a theocracy and become *the* Messiah – for instance 2 Sam: 7: 16; Isa 9: 5–6; Ezek 37: 21–22; Jer 23: 5–6.[59]

Jesus must have been acutely aware of these prophecies and expectations and, therefore, he deliberately acted in such a manner that it amounted to a fulfillment of these prophecies.

It is highly probable and possible that Jesus saw events coinciding with his baptism by John the Baptizer as God's calling to become the savior and king of Israel (Mark 1: 9–11; Matt 3: 13–17; Luke 3: 21–22). The total solar eclipse of 24 November AD 29[60] at about 10:40 local time over Galilee[61] very probably happened when Jesus was baptized and that he saw this as an indication that God

---

[59] Fredriksen, *Jesus of Nazareth,* 124–28.

[60] Gertoux, who compiled a credible chronology of Jesus' life, also places his baptism in AD 29, although he calculated that Jesus was baptized during August (Herod the Great and Jesus, 53.

[61] Although the Gospel of Matthew states that John was baptizing at the river Jordan in the "wilderness of Judea" (Matt 3: 1), John must actually have been in Galilee to the north of Judea at that time since Herod Antipas, the ruler of Galilee, had him arrested shortly after Jesus' baptism – and that could only have happened within Herod's area of jurisdiction (Matt 14: 3; Mark 1: 14; Mark 6: 17; Luke 3: 19–20). It also appears from the chronology in the Synoptic Gospels that Jesus concentrated his ministry initially to Galilee and only appeared in Judea at a later date.

3. JESUS AND HIS CONTEMPORARIES

called him to become *the* Messiah. The report of this event in Mark 1: 9–11, the oldest gospel, must be quoted in full:

> "It happened in those days, that Jesus came from Nazareth of Galilee, and was baptized by John in the Jordan. Immediately coming up from the water, he saw the heavens parting, and the Spirit descending on him like a dove. A voice came out of the sky, 'You are my beloved Son, in whom I am well pleased.'"

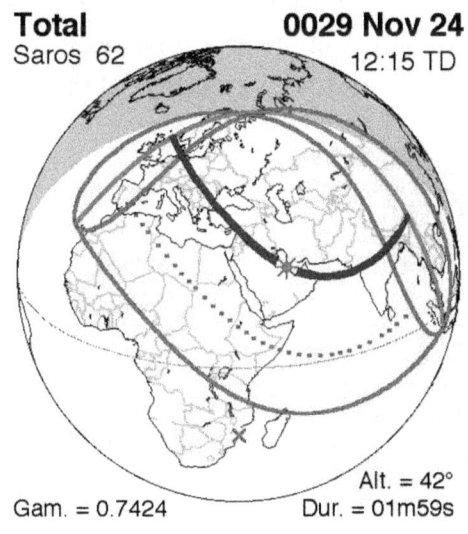

Five Millennium Canon of Solar Eclipses (Espenak & Meeus)

The path of the moon's shadow, where a total solar eclipse was visible, passed through the northern parts of Palestine on 24 November AD 29. The duration of totality was 2 minutes.[62]

All three synoptic gospels report that the heavens were opened directly after Jesus' baptism – most probably the stars in the sky that

---

[62] NASA, Eclipse Website.

3. JESUS AND HIS CONTEMPORARIES

became visible during the day when the light of the sun was blocked by the intervening moon during the eclipse.

It has to be remembered that the ancient Israelites thought that God's heaven was directly beyond the stars and that the stars were actually angels (Neh 9: 6; Job 22: 12–14; Job 38: 4–8; Ps 104: 3; Ps 148: 2–3; Isa 40: 22).[63] In other words: when the stars unexpectedly became visible during day-time it seemed as if the heaven, the abode of God and the angels, was miraculously opened.

During a solar eclipse "a pronounced fall in temperature" is experienced, due to the blocking of the rays of the sun. That causes a wind to blow from the warmer areas outside the path of the moon's shadow to the cooler areas where the heat of the sun is absent.[64]

A computerized reconstruction of the maximum extent of the almost total solar eclipse at 10: 40 local time on 24 November AD 29, as seen from Caesarea-Philippi, north of the Sea of Galilee, when almost 94% of the sun was blocked by the moon. A total eclipse would have been visible further north

That must also have been the case with the eclipse of 24 November AD 29 and people would also have noticed the sudden wind – apart from the appearance of the stars in the sky.

The Greek word for "wind", πνεῦμα (*pneuma*), is also the word used for "spirit", just as the Hebrew word for "wind" is also the word for "spirit" (רוּחַ – *ruach*). For the Jews, therefore, there was no real difference between a spirit and the wind or breath and,

---

[63] Scholtz, *The Prophecies of Revelation*, 30–41.
[64] Encyclopaedia Britannica, "Eclipse: sun".

3. JESUS AND HIS CONTEMPORARIES

therefore, the gospels reported that the (Holy) Spirit "descended" upon Jesus at his baptism (Mark 1: 10; Matt 3: 16; Luke 3: 22) – while it was actually only an unexpected but ordinary wind that blew.

Mark – the oldest gospel – merely reported that Jesus saw the Spirit (or the wind) descending on him *like* a dove or a pigeon (the Greek word may mean both species of birds) – not in the *form* of a dove. Luke 3: 22, though, added that "the Holy Spirit descended in a bodily form" on Jesus.

The Gospel of John (1: 32) states: "John testified, saying, 'I have seen the Spirit [πνεῦμα – *pneuma*] descending like a dove out of heaven, and it remained on him.'" This verse also compares the "Spirit" – or the "wind" – with a dove, without mentioning that a real dove was seen.

It is on account of Luke's description that illustrations of the event usually show a real dove coming down upon Jesus. But that is not what the reports in Mark and John said. They only compared the Spirit or the wind with the movement of air caused by the flapping of the bird's wings as it perches upon a person's shoulder or head. If this interpretation is correct, then Jesus would have perceived the unexpected solar eclipse and the blowing of the sudden wind as a direct message from God, declaring him to be God's "beloved Son" – in other words: the king of Israel.

It has to be stressed that the only people ever called the "son of God" in the Old Testament were the kings of Israel (2 Sam 7: 14; 1 Chr 17: 13; 1 Chr 22: 10; 1 Chr 28: 6; Ps 2: 6–7, 12; Ps 89: 26–28) – except for the angels (Job 1: 6; 2: 1; 38: 8). According to John 1: 49, the expressions "Son of God" and "king of Israel" are synonyms.

3. JESUS AND HIS CONTEMPORARIES

It has to be stressed that the people in those days had no explanation for the occurrence of eclipses and they interpreted these as mysterious divine interventions.[65]

The Jewish newspaper Haaretz quoted Rabbi Blitz: "In Jewish tradition, a total solar eclipse is a warning to the Gentiles and a sign of judgment on the nations."[66]

That may also be how Jesus interpreted the event and he must have seen it as a confirmation of his calling to become *the* Messiah and liberator of the Jews.

We can speculate that Jesus and John planned this baptism specifically for that particular day because they, somehow or other, knew of the expected eclipse. Eshbal Ratzon of the University of Haifa has demonstrated that the so-called Astronomical Book of Enoch, part of the Dead Sea Scrolls, explained how to predict lunar and solar eclipses – something the ancient Sumerians, Babylonians, and Greeks could do.[67] It is, of course, impossible to determine whether Jesus and John knew of this book and its contents, or heard that this eclipse was predicted, but their ties with the Qumran community may have made this a possibility.

The constellations of stars that became visible around the darkened sun all proclaimed the same message to Jesus. Knowledge of the constellations was widespread in those days, as is evident from the fact that there are various allusions to Babylonian astrology in the Old Testament and that most of the visions that John of Patmos had and which he described in the book of Revelation, were actually descriptions of the night sky with its constellations and planets during AD 96.[68]

---

[65] Stephenson, "Eclipse".
[66] Haaretz, 19.03.2015.
[67] Ratzon, "The first Jewish Astronomers".
[68] Scholtz, *The Prophecies of Revelation*, 27–41.

3. JESUS AND HIS CONTEMPORARIES

The eclipsed sun appeared just below the constellation of Ophiuchus or Serpentarius, the Snake Catcher. Ophiuchus is traditionally depicted as a man grasping a snake, the constellation of Serpens, the Serpent.

According to Jewish stellar lore, the constellation of Serpens was a depiction of Satan, the Serpent that tempted Eve to eat from the forbidden fruit (Gen 3).[69]

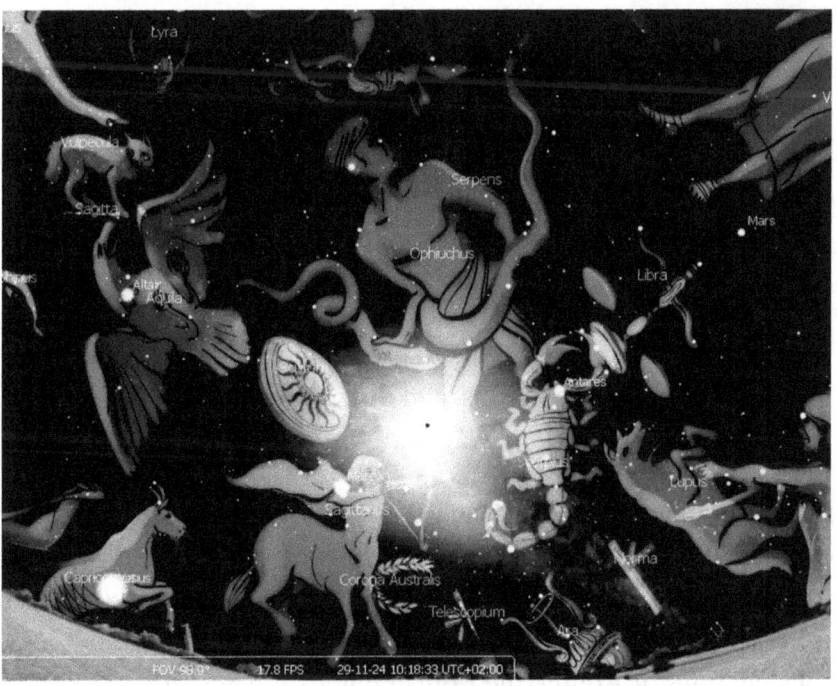

A computerised reconstruction of a part of the sky over Galilee during the solar eclipse of 24 November AD 29, showing the outlines of the stellar constellations.

In Job 26: 12–13 we also read:

---

[69] Allen, *Star Names,* 375.

3. JESUS AND HIS CONTEMPORARIES

> "He stirs up the sea with his power, and by his understanding he strikes through Rahab. By his Spirit the heavens are garnished. His hand has pierced the swift serpent."

The name "Rahab" (רָהַב) denotes a mythical sea monster. The Hebrew word for "serpent" is נָחָשׁ (*Nachash*). It is clear that these two creatures are meant to be one and the same being that resided in "the heavens" – that is, between the stars.

Jesus would certainly have been conscious of these passages in the Hebrew Scriptures, as well as of the significance of the constellation of Serpens. He certainly would have connected that to his calling to become the savior of Israel who was destined to conquer the evil forces of Satan and paganism.

It is likely that Jesus alluded to this vision in Luke. 10: 18:

> "He said to them, 'I saw Satan having fallen like lightning from heaven. Behold, I give you authority to tread on serpents and scorpions, and over all the power of the enemy. Nothing will in any way hurt you.'"

In the computerized reconstruction of the sky at the time of the solar eclipse, it is clear that the constellations of Serpens and Scorpius (the Scorpion) lie next to each other, just above the horizon. Both were regarded by the Jews as representations of Satan[70]. The constellations of Aquila (the Roman Eagle) and Scutum (the Roman Shield) were also hovering on the horizon.[71]

From the perspective of Jesus, on the banks of the Jordan, it must have appeared as if these constellations were about to fall from heaven where they lay just above the horizon. The "lightning" that Jesus mentioned must have been the tiny sliver of the sun still visible

---

[70] [70] Allen, *Star Names,* 362; Scholtz, *The Prophecies,* 189–191.
[71] Allen, *Star Names,* 57.

3. JESUS AND HIS CONTEMPORARIES

behind the moon directly after totality had ended. It also appeared as if the Snake Catcher was trampling upon the Scorpion.

Another important constellation that became visible during the solar eclipse was Capricornus, the Goat. In Jewish stellar lore from the time of Jesus and subsequent centuries, this constellation was named גדיא (*Gadiya*, the kid goat)[72]. That reminds one of the exclamation of John the Baptist after he had baptized Jesus: "Behold, the Lamb of God, who takes away the sin of the world!" (John 1: 29). The planet Venus, the bright morning star, was at that time inside Capricornus, drawing the attention to this constellation. The Hebrew names of this planet was כוכבת (*Kokebet*, the she-star) and מַלְכַּת הַשָּׁמַיִם (*Meleket Hasshamayim*, the Queen of Heaven).

Libra, the Scales (Hebrew: מאזנים – *moznayim*), a symbol of justice[73], lay next to Serpens and Scorpius – conveying the idea that all satanic forces were to be judged by God.

Directly below the occluded sun the constellation of Corona Australis, the Southern Crown or Garland, a symbol of kingship or victory,[74] was visible. This garland was usually associated with the adjacent constellation of Sagittarius, the Archer, usually regarded as a conquering warrior[75] - another symbol of the Messiah.

All these celestial phenomena would have held a powerful message: Jesus, who was baptized on that day, was destined and anointed by God to be the "beloved Son" of God, the Messiah and king of Israel, liberator of his people and conqueror of the Romans. It was, as it were, as if a voice from heaven proclaimed this message.

It is noteworthy that a partial lunar eclipse occurred during the early evening of 9 December AD 29 – exactly a fortnight after

---

[72] Jacobus, "The Zodiac", 318, 323.
[73] Allen, *Star Names*, 273.
[74] Allen, *Star Names*, 172.
[75] Allen, *Star Names*, 352.

3. JESUS AND HIS CONTEMPORARIES

the solar eclipse. Jesus must have been wandering through the desert at that time, struggling with demonic forces (Matt 4: 1–11). Jesus – and those who witnessed the solar eclipse at his baptism – must have seen this partial lunar eclipse as yet another confirmation that he was destined to become *the* Messiah and that delivery from the hated pagan Romans was due.

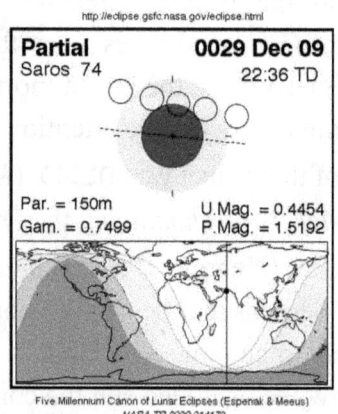

The white areas on this map show the parts of the world where the partial lunar eclipse of 9 December AD 29 was visible. The white circles in the top part of the illustration show how much of the moon was covered by the earth's shadow (the larger dark circle).[76]

What is remarkable about this eclipse, is that the darkened moon lay within the constellation of Gemini and next to the planet Saturn. Gemini, The Twins, with its two bright stars, Castor and Pollux, reminded the Jews of Esau and Jacob, the twin sons of Isaac.[77] Another name for Jacob was Israel (Gen 32: 28).

Shlomo Sela points out, furthermore, that "a special link [exists] between Saturn and Saturday, the holiest day of the week for the Jews". The Hebrew name for this planet is שבתאי (*Shabtai*) – a name connected to the word for "Shabath" – just as there is a

---

[76] NASA, Eclipse Website.
[77] Orlov, *The Atoning Dyad*, 27.

3. JESUS AND HIS CONTEMPORARIES

link between Saturn and Saturday in the English language. Therefore, Saturn can be seen "as the planet in charge of the Jews."[78]

The eclipsed moon within Gemini and next to Saturn would have given Jesus the message that something special was due to happen to the Jews while they watched how their enemies would be darkened or vanquished with their special star protecting them.

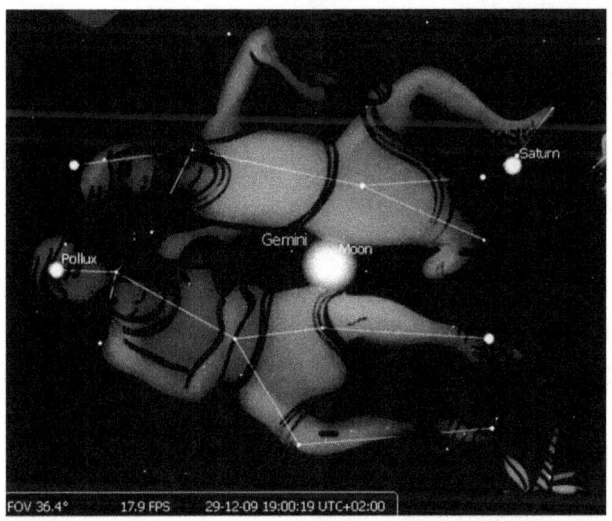

A computerised recreation of the eclipsed moon within the constellation of Gemini with its principal stars Castor and Pollux during the early evening of 9 December AD 29. Saturn is also part of the scene.

Jesus departed for the desert after his baptism and during this time he tried to make sense of the events surrounding his baptism. He reportedly experienced temptations by Satan, but afterwards was cared for by angels (Mark 1: 9–12; Matt 3: 13–4: 11; Luke 3: 21–22; Luke 4: 1–13).

This period of forty days must be greatly exaggerated. Nobody can survive more than ten days without water, especially not in a desert environment in which Jesus experienced these

---

[78] Sela, "Saturn and the Jews".

3. JESUS AND HIS CONTEMPORARIES

temptations.[79] The period of forty days is rather a symbolic number, a reminder of the forty years the Israelites had spent in the desert after escaping from slavery in Egypt. It is also a reminder of Moses who reportedly stayed forty days on the mountain without eating and drinking, while receiving God's commandments (Ex 34: 28).

Anyway, if Jesus fasted for an extended period of time and consequently suffered from malnutrition and dehydration, it is very possible and highly probable that he would have experienced hallucinations with a religious content, in which he struggled with demonic forces, had encounters with angels and which he regarded as a confirmation of his calling from God to establish the kingdom of God in Israel.

The "angels" who cared for him after Satan had left were quite likely desert dwellers who found the disoriented, dehydrated and undernourished Jesus somewhere in the desert and nursed him back to health.

These experiences must have so real for Jesus that he afterwards told his friends and disciples about it – and the compilers of the gospels must have collected these stories from people who heard it from Jesus or from his friends or disciples.

If Jesus was baptised in November AD 29 and he was crucified on 3 April AD 33 (see below), then his public ministry, which started shortly after his baptism, would have spanned somewhat more than three years. During this time, he repeatedly acted as if he was the king-in-waiting of the Jews.

That Jesus was a popular figure and that many regarded him to be *the* Messiah, the savior from oppression, is clear from the gospels. It is repeatedly stated that he drew crowds when he was

---

[79] Craighead and Nemeroff, *The Corsini Encyclopedia of Psychology and Behavioral Science*, 1587; Swaab, *Wij zijn ons Brein*, 247; Encyclopaedia Britannica, "Dehydration".

3. JESUS AND HIS CONTEMPORARIES

teaching, as well as from the following descriptions of his triumphant entry into Jerusalem when he and his disciples attended the annual Passover during April AD 33:

- They brought the colt to Jesus, and threw their garments on him, and Jesus sat on him. Many spread their garments on the way, and others were cutting down branches from the trees, and spreading them on the road. Those who went in front, and those who followed, cried, "Hosanna! Blessed is he who comes in the name of the Lord! *Blessed is the kingdom of our father David that is coming* in the name of the Lord! Hosanna in the highest!" Jesus entered into the temple in Jerusalem." (Mark 11: 7–11 – *emphasis added*).
- On the next day a great multitude had come to the feast. When they heard that Jesus was coming to Jerusalem, they took the branches of the palm trees, and went out to meet him, and cried out, "Hosanna! Blessed is he who comes in the name of the Lord, the *King of Israel!*" Jesus, having found a young donkey, sat on it. As it is written, "Don't be afraid, daughter of Zion. Behold, your *King* comes, sitting on a donkey's colt" (John 12: 12–15 – *emphasis added*).

He entered Jerusalem in this manner on purpose to fulfill a prophecy from the Old Testament:

> "Rejoice greatly, daughter of Zion; shout, daughter of Jerusalem: behold, your king comes to you; he is just, and having salvation; lowly, and riding on a donkey, even on a colt the foal of a donkey" (Zech 9: 9).

Jesus was certainly also aware of the rest of this prophetic utterance of Zechariah, which stated with regards to the king who was to enter Jerusalem on the back of a donkey:

3. JESUS AND HIS CONTEMPORARIES

> "I will cut off the chariot from Ephraim, and the horse from Jerusalem; and the battle bow shall be cut off; and he shall speak peace to the nations: and his dominion shall be from sea to sea, and from the River to the ends of the earth" (Zech 9: 10).

This prophecy promised that the future king of Israel would rule over a huge part of the earth. Jesus clearly relied on this prophecy that God would render the chariots, horses and battle bows of Israel's enemies useless in any struggle.

By upending the tables of the money changers and animal merchants, Jesus followed the example of Nehemiah who threw out the furniture of a certain Tobiah who had taken up residence in a chamber in the temple complex (Neh 13: 7–9). He also referred to Jer 7: 11 to motivate his action: "Is this house, which is called by my name, become a den of robbers in your eyes?" He probably did this to legitimize his claim to be a messiah.

One of the characteristics of Jesus' preaching was that he often called God his "Father" and referred to himself as "the Son (of God)" (Matt 6: 9; Matt 11: 27; Matt 16: 27–28; Matt 23: 9; Matt 27: 54; John 3: 35; John 5: 21; John 6: 46; John 8: 18; John 8: 42 *etcetera*). No prophet of the Old Testament ever did this. Jesus' habit of calling God his Father and describing himself as the son of God was a way of telling the people that he was chosen by God to be the next king of Israel. It has already been shown that the only person in the Old Testament who was ever called a son of God was the Israelite king in Jerusalem (except for the angels) – just as the Egyptian pharaohs regarded themselves as the sons of the god Osiris.[80]

---

[80] Oakes and Gahlin, *Ancient Egypt*, 331.

3. JESUS AND HIS CONTEMPORARIES

Jesus also often referred to himself as the "Son of Man" (Matt 9: 6; 12: 8; 12: 40; 13: 41; 16: 13; 16:28; 24: 27–37; Luke 18: 31 *etcetera*). This expression was taken from Daniel 7: 13–14 –

> "I saw in the night-visions, and, behold, there came with the clouds of the sky one like a son of man, and he came even to the ancient of days, and they brought him near before him. There was given him dominion, and glory, and a kingdom, that all the peoples, nations, and languages should serve him: his dominion is an everlasting dominion, which shall not pass away, and his kingdom that which shall not be destroyed."

This vision in Daniel is clearly a prophecy of the advent of *the* Messiah and Jesus applied it consciously to himself in order to convey the message that he was God's anointed and that he had been called to claim the royal throne.

For Jesus and his contemporaries, politics and religion were inextricably connected; it was not possible to treat them as separate aspects of life.[81] Jesus saw himself as the successor of his ancestor David as king of the Jews. He also thought of the coming kingdom of God as a theocracy on earth since many of his teachings and parables attest that the Jews would be ruled according to the laws of the Old Testament. It is very possible that Jesus remembered the following prophecy of Isaiah regarding this theocracy, which was to be established by *the* Messiah:

> "For to us a child is born, to us a son is given; and the government shall be on his shoulder: and his name shall be called Wonderful, Counsellor, Mighty God, Everlasting Father, Prince of Peace. Of the increase of his government

---
[81] Armstrong, *Fields of Blood*, 123.

3. JESUS AND HIS CONTEMPORARIES

> and of peace there shall be no end, on the throne of David, and on his kingdom, to establish it, and to uphold it with justice and with righteousness from henceforth even forever. The zeal of Yahweh of Hosts will perform this" (Isa 9: 6–7).

He saw himself, therefore, as the earthly representative of God through whom this theocracy was miraculously to be brought about, the Romans driven away and the dynasty of David restored.

Jesus' core message was an echo of that of John the Baptist: "Repent, for the Kingdom of Heaven is at hand!" (Matt 3: 2; Matt 4: 17). Jesus proclaimed the "gospel [good news] of the Kingdom" throughout his ministry (Matt 9: 35; Matt 24: 14).

Many Christians through the ages interpreted Jesus' message regarding the Kingdom of God or Heaven, as reported in the gospels, as pertaining to a state of affairs in the far future after Judgment Day and to the heavenly bliss promised to the faithful in the afterlife. It was supposed to be a spiritual kingdom. The Heidelberg Catechism declares that the Kingdom of God is also to be found wherever people submit to the authority of God through his word and his Spirit, as well as where the works of Satan are destroyed in this world and in the world to come (Q & A 123) – which also amounts to a spiritual kingdom.

That was not how Jesus saw the Kingdom of God or Heaven. There are various instances reported where he clearly stated that the (political) Kingdom was at hand and that those who were alive at that time would not see death before the Kingdom was re-established (Matt 16: 27–28; Matt 24: 34; Matt 26: 29, 64; Mark 9: 1; Mark 13: 20; Luke 9: 27; Luke 21: 32). His disciples and some Pharisees had the clear expectation that he would restore the Israelite kingdom in the immediate future (Luke 17: 20; Luke 19: 11; Acts 1: 6). There were people who wanted to "take him by force, to make him king" (John 6: 15). He taught his disciples to pray to God: "May

3. JESUS AND HIS CONTEMPORARIES

your kingdom come. May your will be done, as in heaven, so on earth" (Matt 6: 10). They had, therefore, to pray for an earthly kingdom in the present.

Joseph of Arimathea, a member of the Jewish Council and who laid the body of Jesus in his family tomb after the crucifixion, "was himself waiting for the kingdom of God" (Mark 15: 43; Luke 23: 51).

We read the following when Jesus recruited Nathaniel as a disciple:

> "Nathanael answered him, 'Rabbi, you are the Son of God! You are King of Israel!' Jesus answered him, 'Because I told you, I saw you underneath the fig tree, do you believe? You will see greater things than these.' He said to him, 'Most assuredly, I tell you, hereafter you will see heaven opened, and the angels of God ascending and descending on the Son of Man'" (John 1: 49–51).

This certainly means that Jesus expected that his experience at his baptism, when the heaven was opened and the stars – in other words, angels – miraculously appeared, to be repeated at some other time.

Jesus regarded the fact that he was able to cast out demons as a proof that the Kingdom of Heaven was due to be established at any moment (Matt 12: 28). Jesus saw himself as the legitimate heir to the throne of David. For that reason, he entered Jerusalem a few days before his execution on the back of an ass to fulfill the prophecy of Zechariah, while enjoying the adulation of the crowds – as pointed out previously. The enthusiastic crowds greeted him specifically as the "son of David" (Matt 21: 1–11, 15; Mark 11: 1–11; Luke 19: 29–44).

He confirmed that he was indeed the king of the Jews when questioned by Governor Pontius Pilate (Matt 27: 11; Mark 15: 2;

3. JESUS AND HIS CONTEMPORARIES

Luke 23: 3; John 18: 33) and, therefore, the Roman soldiers afterwards mocked him as a quasi-royal figure by placing a crown of thorns upon his head (Mark 15: 16–18; John 19: 1–2).

Jesus saw it as his mission to be the liberator and king specifically of Israel, including the ten lost tribes that were exiled and thereafter disappeared after the fall of Samaria in 722 BC. Paula Fredriksen declares, "His mission was a mission to *Israel.*"[82]

To a Canaanite woman, whom he initially refused to help, he declared: "I wasn't sent to anyone but the lost sheep of the house of Israel" (Matt 15: 24). He told his disciples, "Most assuredly I tell you, that you who have followed me, in the regeneration when the Son of Man will sit on the throne of his glory, you also will sit on twelve thrones, judging the twelve tribes of Israel" (Matt 19: 28). In other words, they were supposed to become judges or leaders of the restored nation of Israel, just as the judges of whom we read in the book of Judges, including Samson, Gideon and Samuel. They would, in effect, become Jesus' cabinet ministers or councilors.

When he sent his twelve apostles to spread his message and heal the sick, he gave them the following instructions:

> "Don't go among the Gentiles, and don't enter into any city of the Samaritans. Rather, go to the lost sheep of the house of Israel. As you go, preach, saying, 'The Kingdom of Heaven is at hand'" (Matt 10: 5–7)."

We read in Matt 25: 31 that he told his disciples: "But when the Son of Man comes in his glory, and all the holy angels with him, then will he sit on the throne of his glory" (see also Mark 8: 38; Mark 14: 62; Luke 9: 26; Luke 22: 69; John 1: 51). Jesus, therefore, had the sadly misguided expectation that he would be able to overthrow the

---

[82] Fredriksen, *Jesus of Nazareth*, 238.

3. JESUS AND HIS CONTEMPORARIES

might of Rome with the help of God and a host of angels and re-establish the Israelite theocracy.

This expectation would turn out to be a tragic delusion.

The Romans to be Driven Away

Jesus also told his disciples that Judgment Day and the arrival of the Kingdom would happen in the near future with the help of an army of angels:

> "For the Son of Man will come in the glory of his Father with his angels, and then will he render to every man according to his deeds. Most assuredly I tell you, there are some standing here, who will in no way taste of death, until they see the Son of Man coming in his kingdom" (Matt 16: 27–28).

Jesus, no doubt, found various examples in the Old Testament where God had sent angels to aid the Israelites in their various battles (Ex 12: 29; Ex 14: 19; Judg 2: 1; Judg 6: 11; 2 Sam 24: 16; *etcetera*) and that must have given him the totally false confidence that the battle against the Romans was destined to succeed. Although these reports in the Old Testament must have been legendary or mythological in nature, Jesus – just as his contemporaries – must have taken them at face value to be an accurate rendering of history and he staked his future success on them.

Jesus, certainly, must also have been inspired by the success of the Jewish revolutionaries under the leadership of Judas Maccabeus and his brothers who managed to throw off the yoke of the Seleucid kings of Syria during the fifties of the second century BC and established an independent Jewish kingdom in Palestine.[83]

---

[83] Encyclopaedia Britannica, "Maccabees".

3. JESUS AND HIS CONTEMPORARIES

Jesus certainly had links to Jewish militant groups of which there were enough in his day. Two of his disciples were Simon the Zealot (or terrorist) and Judas Iscariot (or assassin).[84] Two other disciples, the brothers James and John, the sons of Zebedee, were given the nicknames of "Sons of Thunder", which typified their explosive and aggressive personalities (Mark 3: 14–19). His group of disciples were, therefore, a bunch of armed rowdies who acted as his bodyguard (Matt 26: 51; Luke 22: 49; *etcetera*).

For that reason, Jesus declared: "Don't think that I came to send peace on the earth. I didn't come to send peace, but a sword" (Matt 10: 34). Jesus also instructed his followers: "But now, whoever has a purse, let him take it, and likewise a wallet. Whoever has none, let him sell his cloak, and buy a sword" (Luke 22: 36).

It seems as if Peter took this advice to heart because he tried to defend Jesus with his sword when his master was later arrested (John 18: 10).

The Jews of the time directly before and during Jesus' ministry expected the Kingdom of God to comprise of a huge feast. It is probable that Jesus' last Passover meal with his disciples before his arrest, was meant to be a foreshadowing of, or preparation for this feast.[85] After all, during this meal he declared, "Truly I say to you, I will take no more of the fruit of the vine till the day when I take it new in the kingdom of God" (Mark 14: 25). It is clear that he had the tragic expectation that that day would arrive shortly afterwards.

During this last conversation with his disciples, Jesus gave them a long lecture regarding the coming Kingdom and Judgment Day and he illustrated it with various parables (Matt 24–25).

---

[84] Encyclopaedia Britannica, "Simon the Apostle, Saint"; and "Judas Iscariot".
[85] Fredriksen, *Jesus of Nazareth*, 118–19.

3. JESUS AND HIS CONTEMPORARIES

Christians usually read these parables as if they describe something in the far future when Judgment Day arrives. When one takes the preceding arguments into consideration it becomes clear that Jesus was describing the wonderful peace and prosperity that would descend upon the Jews after the Romans had miraculously been driven away and the dynasty of David had been restored – not long afterwards.

Although the authors of the gospels repeatedly put words into the mouth of Jesus to the effect that he presented himself as the savior of mankind (*e.g.,* Matt 20: 28; Matt 26: 63–64; John 10: 30, 38; John 14: 6–14), one can safely regard these utterances as fiction and a re-interpretation of Jesus' mission as seen from the perspective of a number of decades later. These purported words of Jesus cannot be reconciled with his repeated declaration that he was only interested in liberating "the lost sheep of the house of Israel".

If Jesus really did see himself as the redeemer of man, as God incarnate who had come to save sinners from hell, then he, surely, would have made sure that his message would be passed on to the rest of the world. Jesus, however, did nothing of the sort. We don't have a scrap of paper he wrote and there is no record that he dictated his message and claims to any of his followers to write down. That Jesus did make a huge impact on his followers is clear from the fact the Paul wrote extensively about his interpretation of Jesus' message and that a number of gospels were written decades after his death to preserve memories about him. But Jesus himself did nothing to pass his message on to posterity – which proves that he never thought of himself as the savior of sinners and the greatest benefactor of mankind as a whole. It has to be stressed that he more than once declared that he was only interested in liberating "the lost sheep of the house of Israel."

One reason why we don't have anything that Jesus has written or dictated may be the fact that his movement was initially

3. JESUS AND HIS CONTEMPORARIES

an underground organization. He worked in secret in the beginning to keep out of sight of the Roman authorities.

Only one conclusion can be drawn from all this: Jesus saw himself as the liberator and the king-in-waiting of the restored nation of Israel, the successor of his famous ancestor, King David. If a total solar eclipse occurred at the time of his baptism when the heavens were opened, the stars became visible and a miraculous wind blew over him, it is understandable that Jesus thought of himself as God's instrument to establish a theocracy in Israel.

CHAPTER 4
THE ARREST AND EXECUTION OF JESUS

Core Belief of Christians

The meaning of the death of Jesus on the cross and his resurrection on the third day forms the core belief of traditional Christianity. Believers are convinced that Jesus died a horrible death on the cross in order to save them from the horrors of hell in the afterlife and that he ascended to heaven to prepare a place for them in the presence of God. That is, anyway, what they find in the Bible.

The gospels also tell us that the leadership of the Jews of the time rejected Jesus and planned his death.

But is this what really happened? Many attempts have been made during the last two centuries to reconstruct the events surrounding Jesus' death and to separate "fact" from "fiction" or "propaganda". More or less all of these efforts accepted that Jesus was the victim of a Jewish plot.

The most convincing reconstruction of events regarding the trial and death of Jesus was written by a former minister of justice of Israel and Israeli judge, Haim Cohn. He made an extensive study of the times in which Jesus lived, including the legal systems in use by the Romans and the Jews. He came to the conclusion that the descriptions in the gospels were aimed at vilifying the Jews and whitewashing the Roman governor, Pontius Pilate, with the aim of presenting Christianity to the Roman world after the fall of Jerusalem in AD 70 in as favorable a light as possible. In the process, a distorted picture of what really must have transpired was given.

4. THE ARREST AND EXECUTION OF JESUS

A summary of Cohn's most important findings and conclusions are given in the paragraphs that follow – together with insights from other sources. In certain cases, passages from the gospels are quoted and Cohn's comments are given after that.

Judas Iscariot

The role played by Judas Iscariot in the arrest of Jesus as reported in the gospels seems, according to Judge Cohn, very unlikely. The gospels state that he conspired with the chief priests to lead the temple guards to Jesus to be arrested. He was then to identify Jesus with a kiss (Mark 14: 1; Matt 26: 2). This was definitely not necessary since Jesus was a well-known figure and his actions and movements must have been known to many. He taught daily in the temple where he was observed by a large number of people (Luke 21: 38). When he was arrested Jesus reminded those who came for him:

> "Have you come out as against a robber, with swords and clubs? When I was with you in the temple daily, you didn't stretch out your hands against me" (Luke 22: 52–53).

The reason why the story of Judas' "treachery" was included was to show that it was really the Jewish authorities who sought Jesus' blood – and not the Romans.[86]

Another sign that the reports about Judas in the gospels and Acts did not record real history, is the fact that there are conflicting reports about his end. According to Matt 27: 5, he committed suicide by hanging himself, while Acts 1: 18 informs us that he had an accident by "falling headlong, he burst asunder in the midst, and all his bowels gushed out."

The Arrest

---

[86] Cohn, *The Trial and Death of Jesus*, 80.

4. THE ARREST AND EXECUTION OF JESUS

Although the gospels try to convey the idea that the Jewish leaders were responsible for the arrest of Jesus, there is enough evidence that it was actually the Roman authorities who wanted him. The following verse confirms this:

> "Jesus said to the chief priests, captains of the temple, and elders, who had come against him, 'Have you come out as against a robber, with swords and clubs?'" (Luke 22: 52).

The Greek word used for "captain" is στρατηγός (*strategos*) – the title of a Roman officer, either a tribune or a centurion, or otherwise a magistrate. The Vulgate, the Latin translation of the Bible, translates this word with "magistratus". Whatever the meaning, it is clear that an important Roman official accompanied the arresting party.

In the synoptic gospels, the arresting party is only described as a "crowd" or "a multitude with swords and clubs" (Mark 14: 43; Matt 26: 47; Luke 22: 47). The "swords" imply the presence of Roman soldiers, although they are not mentioned explicitly. The Jewish temple guards with their clubs would not have been allowed by the Romans to carry swords in order to prevent an armed insurrection. The Gospel of John is more explicit. In John 18: 3 we are informed:

> "So Judas, getting a band of armed men and police from the chief priests and Pharisees, went there with lights and with arms."

The Greek word for "band" is σπεῖρα (*speira*), which either denotes a cohort, a Roman unit of about 600 legionaries, a maniple or company of about 100 soldiers, or any detachment of Roman soldiers. This word is also used in John 18:12 and Mark 15: 16. The ancient Latin Vulgate translates this word with "cohort".

4. THE ARREST AND EXECUTION OF JESUS

The Greek word used for "arms" is ὅπλον (*hoplon*) and this refers to instruments of war – not the sort of equipment the Jewish temple guards would have carried. There can be no other conclusion: the group that arrested Jesus included a number of Roman soldiers, together with Jewish temple guards and other Jewish temple officials.

According to John 18: 12, the detachment or cohort was under the command of a senior Roman officer. In Greek he was called a χιλίαρχος (*chiliarchos* – literally, a commander of a thousand troops). The Latin Vulgate translated it with "tribune", usually the commander of a cohort; in other words, an important officer – the equivalent of a colonel or a lieutenant colonel in a modern army.

The warrant for arrest could only have been issued by Pontius Pilate or one of his subordinates on his authority or his instructions, otherwise no Roman soldiers under the command of a senior officer would have been involved. The fact that Jesus was arrested by a contingent of Roman soldiers is a clear indication that the Roman authorities regarded him as a dangerous rebel or revolutionary.[87] After all, we read in Matt 21: 10 that when Jesus entered Jerusalem on the back of a donkey and hailed as a king, "the whole city was thrown into commotion."

The presence of Jewish temple guards and other Jewish officials has to be explained, because they would normally not have been part of a Roman raiding party. Fredriksen is of the opinion the a contingent of temple police had to guide the Roman soldiers who were not familiar with the terrain, since they were normally stationed in Caesarea on the coast and only came to Jerusalem to keep the peace during the festivities.[88]

---

[87] Cohn, *The Trial and Death of Jesus*, 86.
[88] Fredriksen, *Jesus of Nazareth*, 254.

4. THE ARREST AND EXECUTION OF JESUS

According to Cohn, the only explanation is that the leaders of the Sanhedrin must have learnt of Pontius Pilate's intention to arrest Jesus and requested him to allow them to keep Jesus in their custody until the next morning when he had to appear at a trial before Pilate – a request that must have been granted.[89] It might even be that Pilate requested the help of the Jewish authorities to catch Jesus – and that may explain the composition of the raiding party.

If the religious leaders of the Jews really wanted to arrest Jesus, they would not have needed help from Roman officials and soldiers. There were enough temple guards who were quite capable of taking Jesus into custody. The contention of the gospels that the Jewish leaders sought the help of the hated Romans in order to catch Jesus, simply does not ring true.

Before Caiaphas
The gospels contradict each other regarding the events after Jesus' arrest. According to Luke 22: 63–66, Jesus was mocked and humiliated during the night and only taken to the Sanhedrin the following morning. John 18: 13–24 relates that Jesus was initially taken to Annas, the father-in-law of Caiaphas, and afterwards sent to Caiaphas. Mark and Matthew inform us, though, that Jesus appeared before the whole Council directly after his arrest (Mark 14: 53, 55; Matt 26: 57, 59).[90]

The truth seems to be as follows: While under Jewish custody, Jesus was not locked up in a cell but taken to the residence of the high priest, Caiaphas, where the Sanhedrin was gathered on the eve of the feast of Passover. The reason for this could not have been the accusation that Jesus was spreading a dangerous doctrine or that he pretended to be the Messiah. If that were the case, his

---

[89] Cohn, *The Trial and Death of Jesus*, 86–88.
[90] Cohn, *The Trial and Death of Jesus*, 94.

4. THE ARREST AND EXECUTION OF JESUS

disciples would also have been rounded up. That the Roman warrant for arrest only involved Jesus is proof that the Roman governor regarded only him as a potentially dangerous rebel or revolutionary.[91]

It is inconceivable that the Sanhedrin was convened to try Jesus and then hand him over to the hated Romans to be executed on a cross. If Jesus was found guilty in terms of any Jewish law that carried the death penalty he would have been stoned (Deut 13: 10; Deut 17: 5) – and certainly not crucified. The chief priests are reported as telling Pilate that they were not empowered to execute people (John 18: 31), but this is certainly not true. Two executions by means of stoning are reported in the New Testament, namely a woman caught in adultery and Stephen, a leader of the first Christians (John 8: 3–4; Acts 8: 57–60). It is also inconceivable that the Roman governor would have granted a request from the Sanhedrin to execute somebody who only broke certain Jewish laws but did not act unlawfully under Roman law.[92]

That the meeting in Caiaphas' residence could not have been an official trial is borne out by the following provisions in Jewish law:

- Trials had to be held in the temple complex, not in a private home;
- Trials had to be conducted during daylight hours, not at night;
- Nobody was allowed to be tried and executed during a feast;
- The testimony of at least two witnesses was needed to sentence somebody to death (Deut 19: 15) – and no witnesses were asked to testify; and

---

[91] Cohn, *The Trial and Death of Jesus*, 90–93.
[92] Cohn, *The Trial and Death of Jesus*, 96–97.

4. THE ARREST AND EXECUTION OF JESUS

- Blasphemy, which carried the death penalty, only amounted to the disrespectful pronouncement or use of the name of God (Lev 24: 16) – of which Jesus was certainly not guilty.

There must, therefore, have been another reason for the extraordinary meeting of the Sanhedrin in the home of the high priest.[93] If the members of the Sanhedrin really wanted to try Jesus, nothing would have prevented them from keeping him in custody until after the festivities and then convening a proper council meeting according to the law. This they evidently did not do.[94]

There is only one rational explanation for the hastily convened meeting of members of the Sanhedrin: they wanted to prevent the execution of Jesus, a very popular and beloved Jewish teacher and leader, by the hated Romans. It clearly was in the interest of the chief priests to be seen in helping Jesus. If they did nothing there would have been a public outcry by the Jewish population of Jerusalem and Judea, whose support and goodwill the Sanhedrin sorely needed. They could not afford to be regarded as accomplices of the Romans.[95]

How did the high priest try to help Jesus and prevent his execution? The only way was to persuade him not to plead guilty to the charge of high treason on which he was to be tried and to promise to behave in such a manner that such a charge could not stick in future. Should Jesus continue to present himself as a king or a messiah, as he did on the day when he entered Jerusalem triumphantly on the back of an ass, the Romans could retaliate, with dire results for all the Jews.[96]

---

[93] Cohn, *The Trial and Death of Jesus*, 98, 112.
[94] Cohn, *The Trial and Death of Jesus*, 113.
[95] Cohn, *The Trial and Death of Jesus*, 114–16.
[96] Cohn, *The Trial and Death of Jesus*, 118.

4. THE ARREST AND EXECUTION OF JESUS

Jesus was evidently aware of the fact that the chief priests tried to help him out of selfish concerns. He was also not prepared to renounce his convictions, his heritage as a descendant of King David and his claim to be a king and a messiah who was called to establish the earthly Kingdom of God. According to all four gospels, the conversation of the high priest with Jesus dealt mainly with his messianic aspirations, which he would not retract. That must have led the Sanhedrin to despair, as reported in the gospels.[97] We read in Mark 14: 63–64:

> "The high priest tore his clothes, and said, 'What further need have we of witnesses? You have heard the blasphemy! What do you think?' They all condemned him to be worthy of death."

It must be reiterated: Jesus' claim to be a messiah was not blasphemous and did not constitute an offence under Jewish law. The Sanhedrin could, therefore, not pronounce a death sentence upon him.[98] The real reason why the high priest tore his robes must have been a sign of his disappointment in failing to convince Jesus to cooperate and his grief because another Jew was due to be executed by the Romans.[99]

The fact that the evangelists portrayed the events at the high priest's residence as a trial in which Jesus was found guilty of blasphemy can only be ascribed to their ignorance of Jewish law as practiced during the lifetime of Jesus, their experiences with the Jews in their own time, as well as their desire to make the Jews the scapegoats for the death of Jesus.[100]

---

[97] Cohn, *The Trial and Death of Jesus*, 125–26
[98] Cohn, *The Trial and Death of Jesus*, 129.
[99] Cohn, *The Trial and Death of Jesus*, 132–34.
[100] Cohn, *The Trial and Death of Jesus*, 138.

4. THE ARREST AND EXECUTION OF JESUS

The Trial

Jesus was handed over to the Roman authorities for his trial by the governor by some members of the Sanhedrin the next morning. According to John 18: 28 they refused to enter the governor's residence with its court room or Praetorium (Greek: πραιτώριον – *praitorion*):

> "They led Jesus therefore from Caiaphas into the Praetorium. It was early, and they themselves didn't enter into the Praetorium, that they might not be defiled, but might eat the Passover."

Cohn points out that there was no Jewish law that prohibited the Jews from entering the residence of a pagan. It would also not have prevented them from partaking in the Passover. The only conceivable reason why they could not enter the Praetorium was because the trial was held *in camera* and they were not permitted to enter. The sentence was, though, later pronounced outside the palace where the public was allowed:

> "When Pilate therefore heard these words, he brought Jesus out, and sat down on the judgment seat at a place called 'The Pavement,' but in Hebrew, 'Gabbatha'" (John 19: 13).

According to Cohn, the name or word "*Gabbatha*" (Greek: Γαββαθα) is unknown in Hebrew or Aramaic – an indication that the author of the Gospel of John didn't know Hebrew or Aramaic.[101]

The gospels mention several conversations Pilate purportedly had with the Jews for which he repeatedly left the courtroom or Praetorium to consult with them outside (Mark 15: 6–

---

[101] Cohn, *The Trial and Death of Jesus*, 147-149; Arndt and Gingrich, *A Greek-English Lexicon*, 148

4. THE ARREST AND EXECUTION OF JESUS

15; John 18: 28–33). Cohn declares this to be a "fallacy and fiction". No Roman governor in his capacity as a judge would have humiliated himself by arguing with the rabble before pronouncing a sentence – especially not Pilate whose disrespect and contempt for the Jews are well documented. The only conclusion is that there was, in reality, no mob outside the governor's residence.[102]

It may be added that Pilate, as a haughty Roman official, could certainly not speak Hebrew or Aramaic. He most probably knew Greek, as most educated Romans did. On the other hand, most Jews probably knew no or very little Latin and Greek. A conversation between Pilate and a Jewish crowd was, therefore, simply not possible.

The gospels make us believe that Pilate found Jesus to be innocent. He, nevertheless, allowed him to be executed. Judge Cohn finds this to be unbelievable. If he indeed declared Jesus innocent of any infringement under Roman law, he would simply have set him free – immediately or at a later stage – without letting him be influenced by a mob that allegedly clamored for Jesus to be crucified. It is also highly improbable that the Jews who hailed Jesus as a king and a messiah a few days previously would have demanded his death.[103]

What is more probable is that all Jews, irrespective of religious persuasion, would have felt sympathy for a fellow Jew who was about to be executed by the despicable Roman occupiers of their country.[104]

Another incredible aspect of the gospel stories is the fact that they all mention that the chief priests were present at the trial of Jesus by Pilate. This could definitely not have been the case because

---

[102] Cohn, *The Trial and Death of Jesus*, 151–55, 165.
[103] Cohn, *The Trial and Death of Jesus*, 156–58.
[104] Cohn, *The Trial and Death of Jesus*, 159.

4. THE ARREST AND EXECUTION OF JESUS

it was impossible for them to stay away from the temple on the morning of the preparation for Passover, the most important annual Jewish religious event. Their presence during the festivities was essential.[105]

All the gospels contain the story of Pilate giving the mob outside the Praetorium the choice of freeing either Jesus or Barabbas, according to their custom that a prisoner had to be released during Passover. Cohn contends that there is no independent record of such a custom, apart from what the gospels tell us. It is also inconceivable that Pilate would have been willing to free Barabbas, a convicted terrorist and killer. He had already, according to the gospels, found Jesus to be innocent; so why not just free him? It is also extremely improbable that the (absent) chief priests would have been able to sway the (non-existent) mob to prefer Barabbas over the popular and charismatic Jesus.[106]

At this point, Matthew added the following fateful words: "All the people answered, 'May his blood be on us, and on our children!'" (Matt 27: 25).

These words were utterly abused throughout the centuries to justify anti-Semitism – by the Christian church and even by the Nazis.[107]

Although the gospels endeavor to whitewash Pilate and to put the blame on the Sanhedrin and the Jews for Jesus' death, it is nevertheless clear from the gospels that Jesus was charged with the crime of declaring himself king of the Jews, without the permission of the emperor in Rome. This amounted to the capital crime of *crimen lesae maiestatis,* originally declared to be unlawful by Julius Caesar in 46 BC and affirmed by Augustus in 8 BC. After all,

---

[105] Cohn, *The Trial and Death of Jesus,* 161.
[106] Cohn, *The Trial and Death of Jesus,* 164–66.
[107] Harris, *The End of Faith,* 92–96.

4. THE ARREST AND EXECUTION OF JESUS

according to all four gospels, the first thing that Pilate did when Jesus was brought before him, was to ask: "Are you the king of the Jews?" [These unanimous reports regarding Pilate's question to Jesus seem to be based on fact and the details were probably supplied by one or more of the officials needed for the trial or some of the soldiers who guarded Jesus during the hearing and not by any Jews who would not have been present].

Jesus confirmed that he was, indeed, the king of the Jews and he was, consequently, found guilty of contempt of the emperor and high treason. Jesus, in effect, pleaded guilty with this admission (Mark 15: 2; John 18: 37).[108] A notice to that effect was later affixed to the cross on which Jesus hang (John 19: 19).

Matthew reports that Pilate's wife sent a message to her husband during the trial, pleading with him to set Jesus free on account of a strange dream she had had (Matt 27: 19). Cohn declares this to be pure fantasy. How would the evangelist have heard of this message? Nobody, apart from Pilate and his wife, would have known about her dream – if she indeed had one. Outsiders would definitely not have known of any exchange between them regarding this matter and, therefore, the author of the gospel according to Matthew – or one of his informants – must have made the story up to create the impression that at least some Romans were sympathetic towards Jesus. It is also inconceivable that Mrs. Pilate would have dared to interfere with her husband's duties while trying an important Jewish rebel leader.[109]

An episode mentioned only in Luke involves Pilate, who, after having heard that Jesus was a Galilean, decided to send him to Herod Antipas, the ruler of Galilee and son of Herod the Great, who was also in Jerusalem to attend the Passover (Luke 23: 7–11). It is

---

[108] Cohn, *The Trial and Death of Jesus*, 171–77.
[109] Cohn, *The Trial and Death of Jesus*, 178–79.

4. THE ARREST AND EXECUTION OF JESUS

difficult to find time for this excursion according to Luke's own time frame. He writes that the Sanhedrin only met in the morning. After having found Jesus ostensibly guilty of blasphemy, Jesus was passed on to Pilate. It would have been at least 10:00 before Pilate was finished with Jesus. Jesus was already hanging for a considerable time on the cross at noon. That means that there would have been very little time, if any, to go to Herod and to return to Pilate for the final death sentence.[110]

Moreover, although Jesus was ostensibly already found innocent by Pilate, Herod would have liked to have Jesus executed because he feared that Jesus was a resurrected or reincarnated John the Baptist whom he had beheaded earlier. Nothing would have prevented Herod from having Jesus killed, had he had the opportunity. He, nevertheless, reportedly sent Jesus back to Pilate after a seemingly fruitless interrogation.[111] The only conclusion that one can draw is that Luke – or his source – invented this episode.

Magee's evaluation of the way in which the gospels present the trial of Jesus is certainly accurate:

> "Since the gospels were completed and widely circulated only after the Jewish War, the purpose of the bowdlerizing was clear — Jewish nationalists were unpopular. The result is the bizarre story of the passion in which a monster like Pilate is an angel and respectable religious sects like the Pharisees are demonic."[112]

The Crucifixion

The Gospel according to John contains an impossible statement:

---

[110] Cohn, *The Trial and Death of Jesus*, 180–81.
[111] Cohn, *The Trial and Death of Jesus*, 184–85.
[112] Magee, "Christianity Revealed", 71.

4. THE ARREST AND EXECUTION OF JESUS

> "Now it was the Preparation of the Passover, at about the sixth hour. He [Pontius Pilate] said to the Jews, 'Behold, your King!' They cried out, 'Away with him! Away with him! Crucify him!' Pilate said to them, 'Shall I crucify your King?' The chief priests answered, 'We have no king but Caesar!' Then therefore he delivered him *to them* to be crucified. So *they* took Jesus and led him away" (John 19: 14–16 – *emphasis added*).

According to these words, it is clear that Pilate allowed the Jews and especially the chief priests – who were actually needed at the temple at that time – to execute Jesus. However, a few verses further we read:

> "Then the *soldiers*, when they had crucified Jesus..." (John 19: 23 – *emphasis added*)

This is an example of sloppy editing, which allowed this inconsistency to creep into the narrative. Apart from that, the Jews would never have used crucifixion to execute a guilty person; their laws required death by stoning. John's readers, at least half a century after the events described, would not have been aware of the finer points of Jewish law and they would not have detected this impossible report. John's description, though, would only have served to feed their anti-Semitic sentiments by picturing the Jews as the executioners of Jesus.

Apart from this, it is inconceivable that the Jews, who suffered under Roman rule and longed for a messiah to deliver them, would have exclaimed: "We have no king but Caesar!" (John 19: 15). It has to be remembered that the same Jews hailed Jesus as their king a few days preciously when he entered Jerusalem on the back of a donkey.

4. THE ARREST AND EXECUTION OF JESUS

The unassailable fact is that Jesus was crucified by Roman soldiers after having been sentenced to death by a Roman governor who ordered his arrest. The headstrong, haughty and autocratic Pontius Pilate would never have allowed the Jews to interfere with the whole process.[113]

Most consulted English translations of John 19: 19 inform us: "Pilate wrote a title also, and put it on the cross. There was written, 'JESUS OF NAZARETH, THE KING OF THE JEWS'." Some translations state that the notice on the cross read: "'JESUS THE NAZARENE, THE KING OF THE JEWS".

That is, however, not what the original Greek text said. Jesus was called a Nazorean (Ναζωραῖος – *Nazoraios*), which has nothing to do with the village of Nazareth, as has been explained earlier. In other words: even Pilate knew that Jesus was known as a Nazorean, a member of the sect of the Essenes and possibly a Nazarite.

Another highly unlikely event is described in Mark 15: 29–32 (as well as in Matthew and Luke) –

> "Those who passed by blasphemed him, wagging their heads, and saying, 'Ha! You who destroy the temple, and build it in three days, save yourself, and come down from the cross!' Likewise, also the chief priests mocking among themselves with the scribes said, 'He saved others. He can't save himself. Let the Christ, the King of Israel, now come down from the cross, that we may see and believe him.'"

It is out of the question that any ordinary Jew, who suffered under the Roman yoke, would have reveled in the suffering of a fellow Jew who was being executed by the Romans – especially a well-loved figure, such as Jesus. They would rather have felt the utmost

---

[113] Cohn, *The Trial and Death of Jesus*, 189.

4. THE ARREST AND EXECUTION OF JESUS

sympathy for the hapless victim of the cruel oppressors. It is also unlikely that the chief priests attended the execution – they were needed at the temple at that time.[114]

Mark 15:40 tells of a number of women who watched how Jesus died. It is known that the women of Jerusalem often tried to soften the suffering of those who were crucified by offering them drugged wine to render them unconscious – which proves the sympathy the Jews had with those who were crucified.[115] The fictitious taunting of Jesus by the Jews while he was hanging on the cross was, therefore, merely another effort to picture the Jews in the darkest colors possible.

From the foregoing it is abundantly clear that the reports of the gospels regarding the trial and execution of Jesus are heavily biased against the Jews and in favor of the Romans. It is, nevertheless, clear: Jesus was arrested by a detachment of Roman soldiers and he was condemned to death by a Roman judge after having been found guilty of declaring himself king of the Jews – which amounted to high treason. A notice to that effect was placed on the cross. The Roman soldiers effected the execution. The role played by the Jewish leaders was perhaps not so honorable in all respects, but they seemed, nevertheless, to have tried to aid the popular and beloved teacher, Jesus of Nazareth, in his hour of need.

In order to portray Jesus as a God-like figure, the gospel writers invented miraculous events during Jesus' death. One reads of a mysterious darkness of three hours while Jesus was hanging on the cross (Matt 27: 45). That event could not have been a solar eclipse since darkness during such an event only takes a few minutes (Stephenson, 2010). Besides that, the Passover was always celebrated during full moon when a solar eclipse is impossible.

---

[114] Cohn, *The Trial and Death of Jesus,* 225–26.
[115] Cohn, *The Trial and Death of Jesus,* 222.

4. THE ARREST AND EXECUTION OF JESUS

There is, however, the possibility that the darkness was caused by volcanic vapors and ash blowing over Jerusalem, obscuring the sun. The darkness was accompanied by a violent earthquake "and the rocks were split" (Matt 27: 45, 51). It is well-known that the Mediterranean area is prone to seismic activity and accompanying volcanic outbursts from time to time – and that could have happened when Jesus was hanging on the cross. Gertoux quotes ancient historians who reported that such a darkness did, indeed, occur.[116]

Matthew 27: 51–54 reports furtermore:

"Behold, the veil of the temple was torn in two from the top to the bottom. The earth quaked and the rocks were split. The tombs were opened, and many bodies of the saints who had fallen asleep were raised; and coming forth out of the tombs after his resurrection, they entered into the holy city and appeared to many. Now the centurion, and those who were with him watching Jesus, when they saw the earthquake, and the things that were done, feared exceedingly, saying, 'Truly this was the Son of God.'"

It has to be granted that the Bible contains reports of many miraculous events. The events described above were, though, of such an extraordinary nature that one cannot but regard them to be utterly impossible. A curtain will certainly not tear "from the top to the bottom". When the material of a heavy curtain gets old and frayed a horizontal tear will appear and the bottom part of the curtain will get loosened from the top part. A vertical tear is highly unlikely.

The purported exclamation of the Roman centurion served to convince the Roman readers of the gospel that the first convert to

---

[116] Gertoux, "Herod the Great", 69–70.

4. THE ARREST AND EXECUTION OF JESUS

Christianity after Jesus' death was a Roman officer and that Christianity was, therefore, an acceptable religion for Romans. It is, nevertheless, unclear how the pagan Roman officer would have gained the insight that this Jewish criminal on the cross was actually "the Son of God" – unless he was aware of Jesus' claim to be the king of the Jews and, therefore, God's son. It is possible that he made a remark in this regard, but then it was only to explain the reason for Jesus' execution. It is also unclear how the Jews witnessing Jesus' crucifixion, would have understood the officer's words in Latin.

If a number of departed "saints" really were raised from their graves it would have been such a stupendous event that one would have found reports of it outside the Bible – which do not exist. No other biblical author refers to this alleged episode, either. What could have happened is that some tombs, consisting of caves or tunnels in the hlls or mountains, could have been opened by the violent earthquake and that the corpses became visible – without the corpses being resurrected.

Thomas Paine asked some pertinent questions regarding these resurrected saints: Did they come naked or clothed from their graves? Did they return to their previous occupations and dwellings? Were they welcomed by their families and former spouses? Did they start law suits against those who inherited their properties to regain those? Did they die again sometime later and were they eventually buried again? Matthew is totally silent regarding these pertinent questions and it is clear that his tale contains no truth.[117]

It has already been argued that Jesus thought of himself as the king of the Jews in a literal and spiritual sense who wanted to establish an earthly kingdom of God or theocracy in Palestine – but not as a supernatural being or as God incarnate. Jesus was an

---

[117] Paine, *The Age of Reason*, 121.

4. THE ARREST AND EXECUTION OF JESUS

orthodox Jew of his times to whom it would have been inconceivable that God, the Creator of heaven and earth, would ever transform himself into a mortal human being. Such a thought is nowhere to be found in the Old Testament.

Jesus must have awaited a miracle from God while he was hanging on the cross through which he would be miraculously saved and the hated Romans be driven away. Luke 23: 42–43 reports:

> "And he [one of the criminals crucified with Jesus] said, 'Jesus, keep me in mind when you come in your kingdom.' And he said to him, 'Truly I say to you, today you will be with me in Paradise.'"

Jesus' retort to this dying man is usually interpreted that both of them would arrive in heaven ("your kingdom" and "paradise") that same day after both had died. It may also mean that Jesus still nurtured the hope that he would be saved miraculously from the cross, that God would drive the Romans away with a host of angels and that his kingdom – "paradise" on earth – would be established. The primary meaning of the Greek word for "paradise" (παράδεισος – *paradeisos*) is, after all, a park with trees, a garden or a pleasure ground, and that can be how Jesus pictured the theocracy he expected. "Paradise" is only used in a secondary sense for heaven.

No such miracle occurred and therefore the disillusioned, shocked, traumatized, and terrified Jesus cried out shortly before he died, "Eloi, Eloi, lama sabachthani?" which is, being interpreted, "My God, my God, why have you forsaken me?" (Mark 15: 34).

From the foregoing it must be abundantly clear that the gospels contain a mixture of pious fiction and sober fact. It is, however, possible to separate fact from fiction if the historical background – as known from other sources – is kept in mind and inconsistencies are cleared up. It is also clear that Jesus was a

4. THE ARREST AND EXECUTION OF JESUS

deluded messiah – he expected angels to save him from the cross and that the Kingdom of God would miraculously be established – but nothing happened and he died a horribly painful and cruel death.

The Date of the Crucifixion

It is possible to calculate the precise date and time when Jesus died. Experts used the information given in the gospels, together with astronomical calculations, to determine when the feast of the Passover – always at a full moon – fell on a Friday during Jesus' lifetime. The most probable date and time of Jesus' death is 3 April (14 Nisan) AD 33 at 15:00. Jesus must have been about 35 years old at that time.

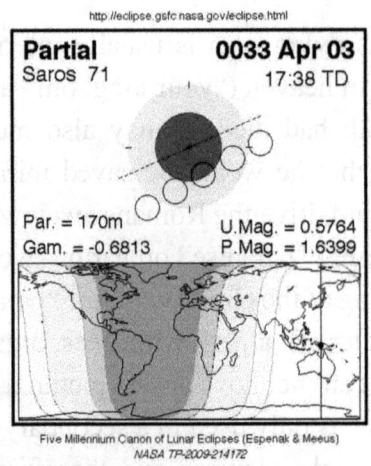

The white areas on the map of the world show where the partial lunar eclipse of 3 April AD 33 was visible. Palestine lies directly on the edge of this area and that means that the partially eclipsed full moon rose over Jerusalem shortly after sunset. The big dark circle represents the earth's shadow that covered most of the moon.

What is remarkable about that date is that a partial lunar eclipse occurred when the full moon rose in the east directly after sunset.[118]

---

[118] NASA, Eclipse Web Site.

4. THE ARREST AND EXECUTION OF JESUS

That may be the reason why Peter alluded to a moon with the color of blood during his speech on Pentecost (Acts 2: 20), seven weeks after the crucifixion.[119] During this speech, Peter quoted from Joel 2: 28–32, including these words: "The sun will be turned into darkness, and the moon into blood, before the great and glorious day of the Lord comes" (Acts 2: 20). The inhabitants of Jerusalem would have had a clear memory when volcanic ash and vapors obscured the sun while Jesus was dying. Peter combined that memory with the memory of the partial lunar eclipse on the same day and many Jews may have explained these events as direct messages from God to confirm that Jesus was indeed *the* Messiah and that the kingdom of God was, after all, due to be established soon.

---

[119] Humphreys and Waddington, "The Jewish Calendar"; Akin, "7 Clues"; Young, "How Lunar Eclipses Shed Light"; Gertoux, "Herod the Great", 67.

CHAPTER 5

JESUS' RESURRECTION, ASCENSION, AND PREDICTIONS

Jesus' Resurrection

It is a Christian article of faith that Jesus survived his death on the cross and his burial by being resurrected and later ascending into heaven. When all the descriptions in the New Testament of these events are examined with an open mind it becomes clear that this article of faith must be relegated to the realm of myths.

How is the resurrection of Jesus Christ to be regarded? Was it really a case where a man who died from his horrible wounds and a serious loss of blood managed to cheat death and was resurrected about 60 hours afterwards? Or is this only a story, which was in line with popular beliefs of the days in which the New Testament was written where myths of dying and resurrected deities – for instance, ancient Middle Eastern and Greek gods such as Baal, Melqart, Adonis, Eshmun, Tammuz, Ra, and Osiris – were well known?[120]

There is no consistency in the reports regarding the resurrected body of Jesus in the New Testament. Paul wrote that Jesus was resurrected with a "heavenly body" or a "spiritual body" – whatever that means (1 Cor 15: 44–55). Likewise, 1 Pet 3: 18 declares that Christ was "put to death in the flesh, but made alive in the spirit" – in other words, he was resurrected only spiritually.

It is probable and possible that Paul thought of this "spiritual body" as composed of a fifth element, the so-called quintessence – apart from the four "ordinary" elements, namely fire, air, water and

---

[120] Encyclopaedia Britannica, "Resurrection".

5. JESUS' RESURRECTION, ASCENSION AND PREDICTIONS

earth – of which the celestial or astronomical bodies were supposed to be made, according to the Greek philosopher Aristotle.[121]

When discussing Christ's resurrection from the grave, which is supposed to be the guarantee that the faithful will also be resurrected, Paul added (1 Cor 15: 40–42, 48):

> "There are also celestial bodies, and terrestrial bodies; but the glory of the celestial differs from that of the terrestrial. There is one glory of the sun, another glory of the moon, and another glory of the stars; for one star differs from another star in glory. So also is the resurrection of the dead. It is sown in corruption; it is raised in incorruption. (. . .) As is the one made of dust, such are those who are also made of dust; and as is the heavenly, such are they also that are heavenly."

One can only conclude that Paul thought of the resurrected "spiritual body" of Jesus as a "heavenly body" – composed of the same stuff as the sun, moon and stars, which differs from the "dust" of our earth and with which he could ascend into heaven, between or beyond the stars (Eph 4: 10).

The gospels, on the other hand, depict Jesus' resurrected body as an ordinary material object of flesh and blood. When Jesus appeared to Mary Magdalene and the other Mary, he spoke to them and they grasped his feet (Matt 28: 9). According to John 21: 9–15, Jesus prepared a fire and roasted some fish, which he ate with his disciples – something an immaterial or ethereal spiritual being supposedly cannot do.

We may also ask: did Jesus appear naked or clothed after his resurrection? After all, the disciples found his burial cloth lying in the tomb after he had disappeared (John 20: 7). If he appeared clothed, then where did he suddenly obtain these clothes?

---

[121] Aristotle, *On the Heavens*, Book 1: 9.

5. JESUS' RESURRECTION, ASCENSION AND PREDICTIONS

Paul's description of Jesus' resurrection differs substantially from the gospels:

> "For I delivered to you ... that he was raised on the third day according to the Scriptures, and that he appeared to Cephas, then to the twelve. Then he appeared to over five hundred brothers at once, most of whom remain until now, but some have also fallen asleep. Then he appeared to James, then to all the apostles, and last of all, as to the child born at the wrong time, he appeared to me also" (1 Cor 15: 3–8).

What is remarkable about this list, is that Paul nowhere mentions the women to whom Jesus was supposed to have appeared first. We are also left in the dark who "all the apostles" exactly were. The gospels and Acts know nothing of a crowd of 500 men to whom Jesus was also supposed to have appeared. If such an important event has really happened, then one could have expected the gospels and Acts to have given more details, which they don't – unless this is a skewed report of the outpouring of the Holy Spirit on Pentecost (Acts 2).

All these diverging and even irreconcilable descriptions of Jesus' resurrection forces any rational investigator to conclude that no real resurrection could have taken place. It will later be shown that, in Paul's case, the appearance of the resurrected Jesus Christ was most probably a case of hallucination.

Jesus' Ascension into Heaven

The gospels and Acts also do not agree about Jesus' ascension into heaven, either. According to Acts, the resurrected Jesus requested that his disciples do not leave Jerusalem. His purported ascension, accordingly, also took place somewhere in or near Jerusalem (Acts 1: 4, 12). Luke also informs us that the disciples stayed in Jerusalem

5. JESUS' RESURRECTION, ASCENSION AND PREDICTIONS

and that Jesus led them from there to Bethany, a village about three kilometers from Jerusalem, whence he rose up into the sky (Luke 24: 33, 50).

The oldest manuscripts of Mark do not contain a story about Jesus' appearances to his disciples and of his ascension; we are only told that his grave was empty. An angel at the empty grave, nevertheless, told the women who came to the grave to tell the disciples that Jesus would meet them in Galilee – not Jerusalem (Mark 16: 5–7). Matt 28: 16, on the other hand, states that Jesus appeared for the last time to his disciples on a mountain in Galilee, far to the north of Jerusalem.

John contains no report of Jesus' ascension. He does tell us, though, that Jesus had a last meeting with the disciples at the sea of Tiberias – far from Jerusalem and also not on a mountain in Galilee (John 21: 1).

These discrepancies and contradictions, together with the cultural background of the times, make the reports of Jesus' ascension highly suspect and they have a clear mythological slant. One can only conclude that the various stories of Jesus' resurrection and ascension cannot be taken seriously; they are definitely not based on any real historical events.

Bishop Tom Wright, who argued that Jesus really did get resurrected, nevertheless admits that the Jews from the Old Testament never believed that the Messiah would be killed and, therefore, the Old Testament doesn't contain any allusions to the resurrection of the Messiah.[122] If this is correct, then Paul had it wrong when he wrote:

> "For I delivered to you first of all that which also I received: that Christ died for our sins according to the Scriptures, that

---

[122] Wright, *The Self-Revelation of God"*, 199.

5. JESUS' RESURRECTION, ASCENSION AND PREDICTIONS

he was buried, that he was raised on the third day according to the Scriptures…" (1 Cor 15: 3–4).

Similarly, John 20: 9 argues that the disciples didn't understand the Scriptures when they discovered the empty grave. John fails, though, to inform us which Scriptures were meant. According to Luke 24: 27 the resurrected Jesus explained to two of his followers on the road to Emmaus what the Scriptures supposedly foretold his death and resurrection. We are, unfortunately, given no details about which passages in the Old Testament purportedly predicted his resurrection.

The truth is, actually, that the Old Testament is silent about any resurrection from the grave of the Messiah. It has been claimed in Acts 13: 35–37 that Ps 16: 10–11 foretold the resurrection of Jesus. This is a fallacy. David, the poet of this Psalm, merely expresses his faith that God will not let his soul perish in Sheol, the realm of the dead. The Messiah of later centuries is nowhere mentioned or implied.

One may, furthermore, ask: Why did Jesus purportedly appear only to his followers and not also to the high priest and the members of the Sanhedrin or to Pontius Pilate? If he had done so, nobody would have been able to doubt his resurrection.

Predicting the Future

The synoptic gospels, Mark, Matthew and Luke, all contain purported predictions by Jesus that Jerusalem with its temple would be utterly destroyed, that great hardships and tribulations had to be expected, that false messiahs and false prophets would lead the people astray and that unusual celestial phenomena would occur.

These predictions were linked to Jesus' teachings about Judgment Day in which he warned his followers to expect this terrible day to arrive at any time soon and to be ready to flee from

5. JESUS' RESURRECTION, ASCENSION AND PREDICTIONS

Judea when they heard of "wars and rumors of wars" (Mark 13: 1–19; Matt 23: 37–39; Matt 24: 1–22; Luke 21: 5–24).

There are two reasons why it can be stated that Jesus never made these predictions and that the author of Mark – or his source(s) – made it all up:

- The first reason is that when it is kept in mind that Jesus was convinced that he was God's chosen Messiah to restore a theocracy in Israel and to drive the hated Romans away it does indeed seem strange that he would warn his followers that the destruction of the temple and the city of Jerusalem was imminent. After all, Jerusalem as the City of David was supposed to be the capital of the restored kingdom of Israel!
- The second reason is that it is clear from Mark 13: 20 that the author of this gospel actually described history – and not a genuine prediction about the future – since in his carelessness, he inadvertently used the past tense instead of the future tense in this verse: "And if the Lord *had* not made the time short, no flesh would have been kept from destruction; but because of the saints he *has* made the time short" (*own emphasis*). Matthew, who copied these words, deliberately changed the past tense in this sentence to the future tense to fit the pretense that Jesus had predicted these events forty years earlier – instead of describing a real event from the past (Matt 24: 22).

The only conclusion that can be drawn is that the authors of the gospels put these words in Jesus' mouth after the temple had been destroyed during the Jewish War in August AD 70 and they then presented Jesus as a prophet who had foreseen all this. The destruction of the temple did happen as Jesus purportedly had predicted: there was a bloody war, the temple was totally destroyed

5. JESUS' RESURRECTION, ASCENSION AND PREDICTIONS

and not one stone was left standing on the other, while Jesus' followers in Jerusalem and Judea really did flee.[123]

Flavius Josephus, the Jewish historian, gave a detailed description of the Jewish War of AD 66–70. He wrote especially in Book VI of his work *The Wars of the Jews* (completed about AD 78) about conditions within Jerusalem during the siege, how the city was taken by the Roman legions and how the temple went up in flames. The Romans crucified thousands of prisoners, while others were taken into slavery. Before the fall of the city, there were various prophets and "deceivers" proclaiming that God would never allow his holy city to be taken by pagans. When famine broke out after the city had been encircled by the Roman legions, civil war broke out within the city and looters terrorized the trapped population. The military leaders were at loggerheads with each other and some hotheads even denounced their own family members as traitors. In the end, the defenders of the city were so weakened by infighting that the Roman soldiers easily breached the last defenses and razed the city. Only three towers of the whole city were left standing.

It is clear that Josephus' description tallies to a remarkable extent with Jesus' "predictions". The only explanation is that the author of Mark drew on his own knowledge of events to fabricate a prophecy attributed to Jesus and that Matthew and Luke repeated his story, with some embellishments of their own.

---

[123] Eusebius, *Historia Ecclesiastica,* Liber III/VIII/2); Encyclopaedia Britannica, "Jewish Revolt, First".

5. JESUS' RESURRECTION, ASCENSION AND PREDICTIONS

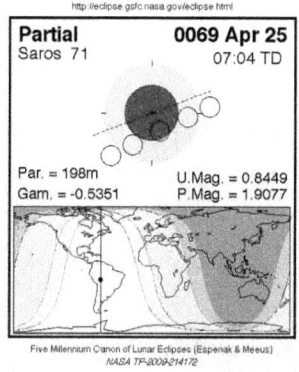
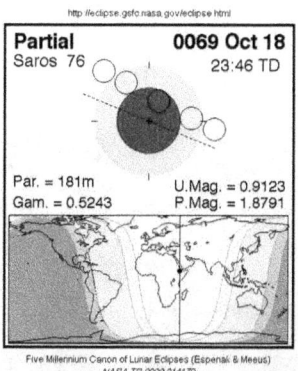

The white parts on these maps show the parts of the earth where two near-total lunar eclipses occurred during the Jewish War. The maximum extent of the first eclipse occurred shortly before sunrise and the second eclipse happened at about 23:00 local time, as seen from Jerusalem.

The gospels mention that Jesus allegedly also predicted:

> "But in those days, after that oppression, the sun will be darkened, the moon will not give her light, the stars will be falling from the sky, and the powers that are in the heavens will be shaken" (Mark 13: 24–25).

Josephus and Eusebius of Caesarea both reported that a comet was to be seen in the sky for almost a whole year during the war.[124] There were two almost total lunar eclipses a few months before the siege of Jerusalem started in March AD 70 – as shown on the illustrations above.

In addition, several meteor showers (shooting stars) were visible during the second lunar eclipse, as shown on the simulation of the night sky over Jerusalem at the height of the lunar eclipse in October AD 69 when the glare of the full moon was greatly diminished. Meteor showers are caused by the earth moving through

---

[124] Josephus: *War*, Liber VI/V/3; Eusebius, Liber III/VIII/2

5. JESUS' RESURRECTION, ASCENSION AND PREDICTIONS

the debris left by passing comets and when bits of this debris burn out when they hit the earth's atmosphere.

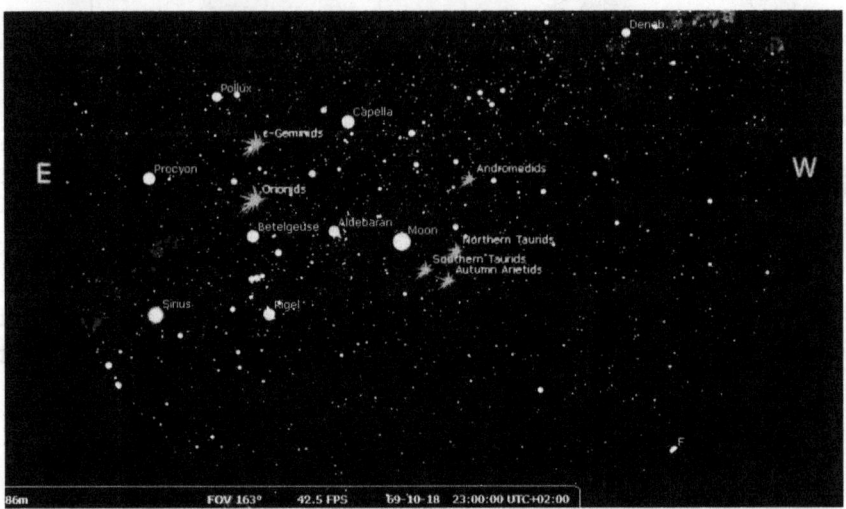

A computerized recreation of the night sky over Jerusalem on 18 October AD 69 at 23:00 when the full moon was almost totally eclipsed. Several meteor showers were observed at that time, namely the ε-Geminids, the Orionids, the Andromedids, the Northern Taurids, the Southern Taurids and the Autumn Arietids.

During the early morning before the destruction of the temple on 30 August AD 70, the planets Venus, Jupiter and Mercury (regarded as pagan deities) lay in a straight line within the constellation of Leo [the Lion – the sign of the tribe of Judah (Gen 49: 9 and Rev 5: 5)] on the eastern horizon, as seen from Jerusalem. In addition, Mars or the pagan god of war, was a threat in Cancer (the Crab), that was ready to pounce upon the Lion with its claws.

A conjunction between Venus and Jupiter occurred four days previously when they formed a single bright object in the sky just before dawn. The last few defenders of Jerusalem, as well as their Roman attackers, must have noticed these unusual alignments and concluded that the fate of Jerusalem and Judea was sealed.

5. JESUS' RESURRECTION, ASCENSION AND PREDICTIONS

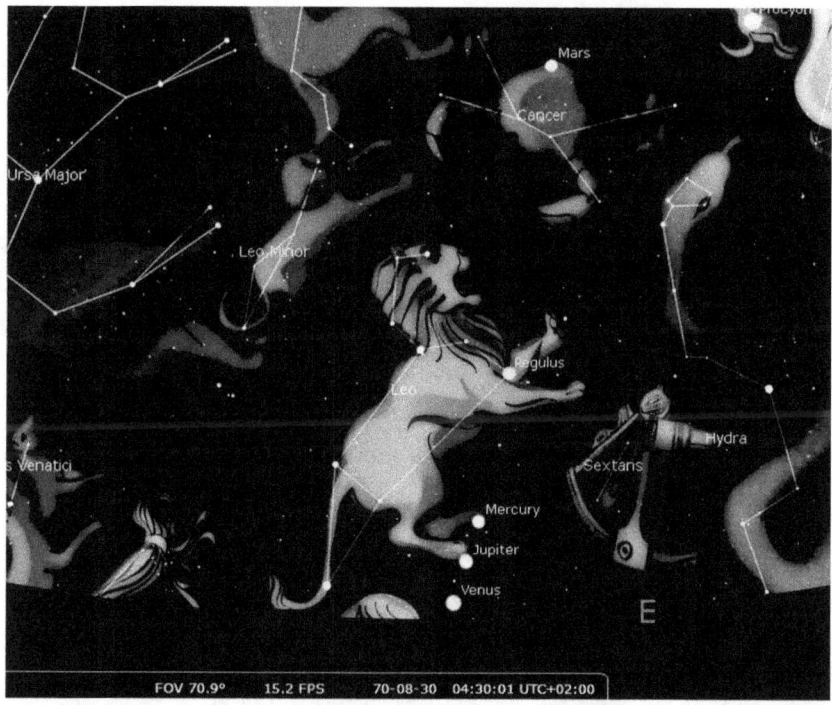

A computerized recreation of the stars, planets and constellations just above the eastern horizon during the early morning of 30 August AD 70 at 04:30, as seen from Jerusalem, the day on which Jerusalem was conquered by the Romans.

From their knowledge of astrology – which was widespread in those days, as has been pointed out previously[125] – they would have drawn the conclusion that the gods of Rome were poised to deal the Lion of Judah a fatal blow.

Mark 13: 25 also referred to "the powers that are in the heavens"; that must have been an allusion to these celestial phenomena (see also Matt 24: 29 and Luke 21: 26).

To complicate matters, a partial solar eclipse was visible from Jerusalem on 20 March AD 71, a few months after the

---

[125] Malina, *On the Genre and Message of Revelation*; Jacobus, "The Zodiac"; Scholtz, *The Prophecies of Revelation*.

5. JESUS' RESURRECTION, ASCENSION AND PREDICTIONS

destruction of Jerusalem, which occurred on 30 August AD 70 – just as Mark 13: 24 proclaimed that *"after* that oppression [the destruction of Jerusalem], the sun will be darkened…" (*emphasis added*).

With the total lack of knowledge of celestial mechanics in those days, it is understandable that the superstitious people of those times, who were all convinced of the "truths" of astrology, would have seen these signs in the heavens as evil omens linked to the destruction of Jerusalem and the defeat of the Jews.

Stephenson noted: "Eclipses of the Sun and Moon are often quite spectacular, and in ancient and medieval times they were frequently recorded as portents — usually of disaster."[126]

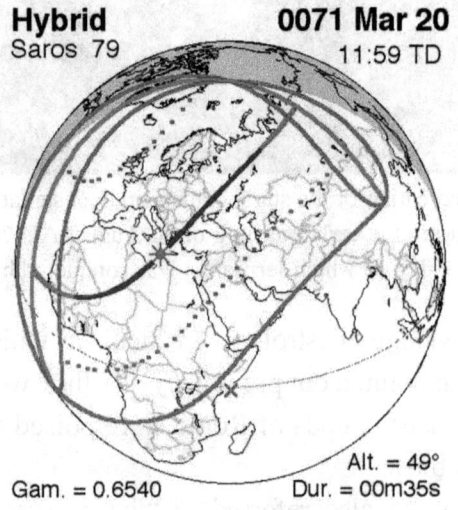

Solar eclipse, 20 March AD 71. The path of the shadow of the moon, eclipsing the sun, is shown where it started in Siberia and ended in West Africa. Totality could have been seen in Greece, but only a partial eclipse was visible in Judea. Totality was reached at 11:24 in Athens.

---

[126] Stephenson, "Eclipse."

5. JESUS' RESURRECTION, ASCENSION AND PREDICTIONS

Delsemme added: "In ancient times, without interference from streetlights or urban pollution, comets could be seen by everyone. Their sudden appearance — their erratic behavior against the harmonious order of the heavenly motions — was interpreted as an omen of nature that awed people and was used by astrologers to predict flood, famine, pestilence, or the death of kings."[127]

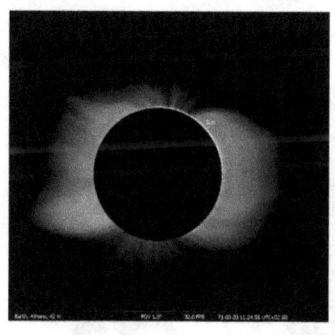

A computerized reconstruction of the total solar eclipse over Athens in Greece on 20 March AD 71 at about 11:24 local time when 99,9% of the sun's surface was covered by the moon.

The author of the Gospel of Mark, who wrote during the seventies of the first century AD – in other words, after the destruction of Jerusalem – would have had knowledge of these frightening celestial phenomena and he included them in the purported predictions of Jesus in order to portray him as a great prophet and to enhance his reputation.

One may even speculate that the author of the Gospel of Mark was in Greece at the time of the solar eclipse of 20 March 71 AD at a location where the eclipse was total and that prompted him to write that "the sun will be darkened" – not realizing that the destroyed Jerusalem was experiencing only a partial eclipse on that date.[128]

---

[127] Delsemme, "Comet".

[128] There is no unanimity about the date of the Gospel of Mark. The fact that Mark mentioned the eclipse of 20 March AD 71 is a clear indication

5. JESUS' RESURRECTION, ASCENSION AND PREDICTIONS

The fact that Mark could have been in Greece (perhaps Athens, Ephesus or Thessalonica) when he composed his gospel, may have contributed to his decision to write his book in Greek for a Greek-speaking readership – and not in Hebrew, Aramaic or Latin. Mark must have thought that it was not possible for Jesus not to have foreseen all these disasters and celestial signs and, therefore, he invented the words ascribed to Jesus in the light of the known history of the Jewish War and his own observations of the eclipses.

Vespasian and Titus, the Roman generals and later emperors who vanquished the Jews during the war of AD 66–70.

The words of Mark were copied by Matthew and Luke and they added to them. It is, nevertheless, clear that Jesus never predicted the Jewish War, the destruction of Jerusalem and its temple and the accompanying celestial phenomena.

It has, in addition, to be pointed out that Judgment Day and Jesus' second coming did not coincide with the destruction of Jerusalem and the temple as Jesus purportedly had predicted.

---

that the final version of this gospel could not have been completed earlier than this date.

CHAPTER 6

VIEWS OF THE ORIGINAL CHRISTIANS REGARDING JESUS

The Jesus Movement

The conventional Christian view is that Jesus never envisaged the founding of the Christian Church and that the church was only born on the day of Pentecost when the Holy Spirit was poured out on the assembled followers of Jesus in Jerusalem, a few weeks after his death.

It is clear, though, that Jesus did start at least a movement or party within Judaism – parallel to other movements and parties of his time, such as the Sadducees, Pharisees, Zealots and the followers of John the Baptist. One can characterize this party as a kingdom party or monarchy party. When Jesus sent his disciples out on a recruiting drive for his movement, he instructed them as follows:

> "Don't go among the Gentiles, and don't enter into any city of the Samaritans. Rather, go to the lost sheep of the house of Israel. As you go, preach, saying, 'The Kingdom of Heaven is at hand.'" (Matt 10: 5–7).

Jesus certainly thought of organizing his followers. For instance, we read in Matt 16: 16–19 –

> "Simon Peter answered, 'You are the Christ, the Son of the living God.' Jesus answered him, 'Blessed are you, Simon Bar-Jonah, for flesh and blood has not revealed this to you, but my Father who is in heaven. I also tell you, that you are

6. VIEWS OF THE ORIGINAL CHRISTIANS REGARDING JESUS

> Peter, and on this rock I will build my assembly, and the gates of Hades will not prevail against it. I will give to you the keys of the Kingdom of Heaven..."'

This passage in the Gospel of Matthew seems to preserve a memory that Jesus thought of his followers as an "assembly" and that this assembly would have as its motto or "rock" that Jesus was the son of the living God – in other words: the promised king of Israel. Peter was given the promise that he would be one of the leading figures in this movement or "assembly" and that this "assembly" would herald in the (earthly) Kingdom of Heaven, of which Peter was given the keys. That must have led to some jealousy amongst the disciples because they, on occasion, argued amongst themselves who would be the most important in Jesus' kingdom (Mark 9: 33–34).

Jesus also mentioned his "assembly", "congregation", or "gathering" in Matt 18: 17. The Greek word used is ἐκκλησία (*ekklesia*) and its most basic meaning is "an assembly of the people convened at a public place of the council for the purpose of deliberating". It is most probably a translation of the Hebrew word קָהָל (*qahal*) – which was used in the Old Testament for a gathering of the people of Israel with the object of worship, but also in a political sense, namely the whole of the chosen nation belonging to God. Jesus most probably used the word "qahal" when addressing his disciples – which word was then rendered with "ekklesia" in Greek in the gospel. It does seem, therefore, that Jesus thought of some sort of movement or organization comprised of his followers.

He meant this movement to be a restoration of the people of Israel with him as royal sovereign and for that reason he chose twelve disciples or apostles as symbolic representatives of the twelve patriarchs and twelve tribes of Israel.

The word "ekklesia" is used in the rest of the New Testament for the "church" or "congregation" – the gathering of Christians.

6. VIEWS OF THE ORIGINAL CHRISTIANS REGARDING JESUS

This movement or party, largely composed of Essenes or Nazoreans, survived after Jesus' death and eventually his brother James became the leader. The initial leadership was exercised by the twelve apostles and they were assisted by seven men (Acts 6: 1–6) – who later appeared as the body of elders of which we read in Acts 15: 4. This movement appears to have expected the return of Jesus to establish the kingdom of God but the revolutionary fervor of the days of Jesus seems to have evaporated. We are told that even some priests and Pharisees joined this movement, which became known as "The Way" (Acts 6: 7, 9: 2; 19: 9, 23; 24: 14, 22) or "the sect of the Nazoreans" (Acts 24: 5). There may have been several thousand members of this group, who were baptized "in the name of Jesus Christ" when they joined (Acts 2: 38, 41).

After Jesus' execution and disappearance from the scene, his Jewish followers continued to revere him as a messiah and they seemed to have expected his return.

It has already been shown that Jesus was a member or an associate of the sect of the Essenes or Nazoreans. The fact that his followers were also called the "sect of the Nazoreans" (Acts 24: 5) is an indication that a substantial number of Essenes from the Essene Quarter in Jerusalem and elsewhere were members of the Jesus Movement after his death.

The Jewish Encyclopedia explains: "The silence of the New Testament about the Essenes is perhaps the best proof that they furnished the new sect [the followers of Jesus] with its main elements both as regards personnel and views. The similarity in many respects between Christianity and Essenism is striking."[129]

The Jewish Encyclopedia adds that the Nazoreans were a "[s]ect of primitive Christianity; it appears to have embraced all

---

[129] Kohler, "Essenes".

6. VIEWS OF THE ORIGINAL CHRISTIANS REGARDING JESUS

those Christians who had been born Jews and who neither would nor could give up their Jewish mode of life."[130]

Abba Yesai Nasrai even described the Essenes as "[a]n ascetic group flourishing until their mass conversion to Nazorean Christianity in the first century AD."[131]

Moshe Dann posed the question: "Was Christianity the spiritual heir of the Essenes?" He answered this question in the affirmative and pointed out that many of the practices and views of the Essenes were taken over by Christianity[132] – which is no surprise, since many Essenes or Nazoreans were followers of Jesus.

Only two early Christian authors wrote about the Nazoreans: Epiphanius (who was already referred to) and Jerome, the translator of the Bible into Latin. Kinzig notes: "Jerome mentions the Nazoraeans only incidentally in a number of passages scattered across his huge exegetical work."[133] In the light of this, it is actually strange that Jerome consistently translated Ναζωραῖος (*Nazoraios*) in the gospels and Acts into Latin with "Nazarenus" – in other words: "Nazarenes" and not "Nazoreans", with the exceptionof Matt 2: 23 where he rendered this word with "Nazareus".

History knows the Jesus Movement after his death also under the name of the "Ebionites" (Ἐβιωναῖοι – *Ebionaioi*). Bishop Epiphanios wrote that the Ebionites were simply an offshoot of the Nazoreans. He, evidently, didn't know the origin of the name "Ebionites" and he described them as the followers of a certain Ebion who "was of the Nazoraeans' school."[134]

---

[130] Jewish Encyclopedia, "Nazarenes".
[131] Nasrai, "Cherubic Sword".
[132] Dann, "The Essenes".
[133] Kinzig, "The Nazoreans", 464.
[134] Epiphanios, *Panarion*, 30:1(1).

6. VIEWS OF THE ORIGINAL CHRISTIANS REGARDING JESUS

According to the description given by Epiphanios of the doctrine of the Ebionites and the Nazoreans, there were no real differences and these groups may be regarded as actually one and the same.[135] These doctrines were – as it is to be expected – similar to the ideas propagated by the Essenes.[136]

Epiphanios reports that members of both these groups were to be found in his time in the area of Decapolis and Pella, where they fled during the Jewish war of AD 67–70,[137] which confirms that they were actually a single group, known by two names.

Acts and Paul's Epistles

How did the first followers of Jesus view him after his death? Unfortunately, the history of the early church contained in the book of Acts cannot be relied upon since it was written by the same person who was the author of the Gospel of Luke, who gave a highly biased rendering of Jesus' life. The anti-Semitism as found in the gospels is, for instance, also occurs in Acts 6: 11–7: 60 and 11: 19.

One cannot, either, use the oldest parts of the New Testament, namely the letters of the apostle Paul, as a trustworthy record of how the earliest followers of Jesus regarded him because Paul had different views than those held by the apostles and elders in Jerusalem (Acts 15: 1–34; Acts 21: 7–26; Gal 2). Paul was not an eye-witness of the ministry of Jesus and he only came to the conclusion that Jesus was a divine figure on account of a series of visions and revelations he claimed he had had (Gal 1: 11–19; 1 Cor 11: 23; 2 Cor 12: 1–5; Eph 3: 3).

---

[135] Epiphanios, *Panarion,* 29 and 30; see also: Encyclopaedia Britannica, "Ebionite".
[136] Encyclopaedia Britannica, "Ebionite".
[137] Epiphanios, *Panarion,* 29(7:7), 30(2:7).

6. VIEWS OF THE ORIGINAL CHRISTIANS REGARDING JESUS

There is reason to believe that these visions and revelations were actually hallucinations, which resulted from left temporal lobe epilepsy, a traumatic brain injury or another brain disorder – as will be argued in the next chapter.

The Document "Q"

The oldest record we have of Jesus is contained in a lost document, nowadays called "Q". It is, however, possible to reconstruct this document.

There is consensus between scholars of the New Testament that the Gospel of Mark is the oldest gospel. It is, after all, the shortest. Almost all the contents of Mark are to be found in Matthew and Luke, augmented by other material. One can almost say that Matthew and Luke are expanded re-editions of Mark.

When one compares this additional material in Matthew with that in Luke, it becomes clear that they both incorporated the same older source into their narratives, apart from other material each one of them uniquely utilized. This common older source has been named "Q", derived from the German word for "source", namely "Quelle".[138]

The reconstructed Q is an interesting document. It contains mostly sayings and teachings of Jesus, ostensibly collected from those who heard him during his lifetime. Q does not contain any reports of Jesus' birth, his baptism, his miracles, his trial by Pontius Pilate, his crucifixion or his resurrection. He is nowhere described as God incarnate or as a divine figure. In other words: Q, the oldest record we have of Jesus, portrays him merely as an ordinary human being and as a wise teacher.

---

[138] Mack, *The Lost Gospel*, 18; 71–102; Rylaarsdam et al., "Biblical Literature".

6. VIEWS OF THE ORIGINAL CHRISTIANS REGARDING JESUS

Therefore, the earliest Christians who collected the teachings of Jesus and who must have been members of the Jesus Movement in an around Jerusalem during the first decades after Jesus' death, did not regard him as anything but an ordinary mortal. They held him in high regard and even saw him as a messiah – somebody anointed by God – but it never occurred to them to think of him as the savior of the world or the second Person of a Triune God as portrayed in Paul's letters, in the rest of the gospels, the book of Revelation and in Christian creeds.

We have no extant copies of Q. When its contents were incorporated into Matthew and Luke it was probably deemed unnecessary to keep any copies of this collection of Jesus' teachings.[139]

Teachings of the Ebionites

Information about the Ebionites is scarce and we have to rely on the descriptions given by their critics and opponents. Their name in Hebrew, אֶבְיוֹנִים (*Ebyonim*), describes them as "the poor". Although this name only entered history during the second century AD, they may be regarded as the direct descendants of the first followers of Jesus in Jerusalem, Judea and Galilee.[140]

It is inaccurate to call the Ebionites "Christians" since they never used this name for themselves – they were merely the members of the group of Jewish followers of Jesus after his death.[141] According to Acts 9: 2, 19: 9, 23 and 24: 5, the Jewish followers of Jesus called themselves "The Way" (ἡ ὁδός – *he hodos*) or the "Nazoreans" (Ναζωραῖοι – *Nazaraioi*). In Acts 21: 16, they are simply called "disciples".

---

[139] Rylaarsdam et al., "Biblical Literature".
[140] Jewish Encyclopedia, "Ebionites".
[141] Epiphanios, *Panarion*, 30:2(2).

6. VIEWS OF THE ORIGINAL CHRISTIANS REGARDING JESUS

The Ebionites denied the virgin birth and divinity of Jesus. Epiphanios wrote that they taught that "Christ is the offspring of a man, that is, of Joseph." They, nevertheless, regarded Jesus as a messiah or a person anointed by God[142] – more or less as Jesus was portrayed in Q.

The importance of this group has often been neglected by conventional Christian theologians since they just could not accept that any early followers of Jesus, Jewish or gentile, could really deny his divinity, virgin birth and resurrection from death. It will be shown, though, that these people constituted the first Jerusalem congregation of the followers of Jesus after his death.

It has already been mentioned that the Jews in Jesus' time yearned for a messiah, someone to deliver them from the yoke of foreign domination by the pagan Romans. They found promises in the prophecies of the Old Testament that such a figure would indeed appear. It has to be stressed that these prophecies nowhere taught that the Messiah would be a divine figure, God himself who would appear in human form. The Messiah – there were actually more than one, including King Cyrus of Persia (Isa 45: 1) – was always portrayed as an ordinary human being. The final Messiah was expected to be a king descended from David and a mighty warrior who would free his people from their enemies.[143]

The Ebionites (and Nazoreans), who were Jews and knew the Hebrew Scriptures, would therefore never have expected their Messiah, Jesus of Nazareth, to have a divine nature.

The early Christian theologian, Origen, wrote that "those Jews who have received Jesus as Christ are called by the name of Ebionites" (Ἐβιωναῖοι χρηματίζουσιν οἱ ἀπὸ Ἰουδαίων τὸν Ἰησοῦν ὡς Χριστὸν παραδεξάμενοι – *Ebionaioi chrematizousin hoi*

---

[142] Epiphanios, *Panarion*, 30(3:1).
[143] König, *Die Grot Geloofswoordeboek*, 323–25.

6. VIEWS OF THE ORIGINAL CHRISTIANS REGARDING JESUS

apo Ioudaion ton Iesoun os Christon paradexamenoi).[144] Eusebius, the first Christian historian, equated the Ebionites with the "people of the Church in Jerusalem" (λαός ἐν Ἱεροσολύμοις ἐκκλησίας – *laos en Ierosolymois ekklesias*).[145]

Eusebius also informs us that the leader of the followers of Jesus in Jerusalem after his crucifixion was James, the brother of Jesus (*cf* Acts 15: 13; Acts 21: 18; Gal 1: 19). He was succeeded by Symeon, "a cousin of the Savior" (ἀνεψιός τοῦ σωτῆρος – *anepsios tou soteros*) and he, in turn, was succeeded by other relatives of Jesus after he had been martyred, including a nephew called Judas.[146] These leaders definitely knew Jesus during his lifetime or had relatives who knew Jesus. The fact that brothers and other relatives of Jesus succeeded him as leaders of the Jesus Movement is an indication that some sort of a dynasty was established and that the followers of Jesus constituted a separate sect within Judaism – just as there were other factions, parties or sects in Judea and Galilee, such as the Pharisees, Sadducees and Zealots (Acts 5: 17; 15: 5; 26: 5; 28: 22).

The main difference between the Jesus Movement and other Jewish religious movements was that they regarded Jesus as *the* Messiah and that he would return soon to free the Jews from foreign domination – a view other Jewish groups did not share. The distinction between these sects or groups was not always clear-cut. We read, for instance, in Acts 6: 7 and 15: 5 of a number of priests and Pharisees who were also followers of Jesus.

It is possible that the members of the Jesus Movement in Judea expected Jesus to return as a reincarnated person – just as

---

[144] Origen: Contra Celsum (ΚΑΤΑ ΚΕΛΣΟU), Liber II(1).
[145] Eusebius: Liber III/V/3 and XXVII.
[146] Eusebius, Liber III/XI and XXXII.

6. VIEWS OF THE ORIGINAL CHRISTIANS REGARDING JESUS

Jesus declared that John the Baptist was actually a reincarnation of the prophet Elijah (Matt 11: 13–14; Matt 17: 12–13).

It is reported in Acts 4: 34 that the first "Christians" in Jerusalem lived in poverty and shared their belongings with each other – a sign of their Essene background. This must probably be the origin of the name of Ebionites. This was also how Jesus and his group of disciples lived. He declared that "[t]he foxes have holes, and the birds of the sky have nests, but the Son of Man has nowhere to lay his head" (Luke 9: 58). According to Luke 18: 24–25, Jesus followed the Essenes' condemnation of riches when he declared:

> "How hard it is for those who have riches to enter into the kingdom of God! For it is easier for a camel to enter in through a needle's eye, than for a rich man to enter into the kingdom of God."

We are told in Luke 8: 2–3 of a number of women who followed Jesus and his band of disciples and "ministered to them from their possessions" – just as the Essenes did.

Another reason why the members of the Jerusalem congregation sold all their belongings and shared the proceeds was probably that they expected Jesus' second coming and Judgment Day to arrive very soon and that it didn't make sense to accumulate worldly possessions, which would prove to be worthless on Judgment Day and in the afterlife.

Paul writes in Gal 2: 10 that he was required during his visit to Jerusalem "to remember the poor". This may be an oblique reference to the Ebionites, the "poor" followers of Jesus in and around Jerusalem. In 1 Cor 16: 3 and 2 Cor 8: 4 we are told that Paul collected money for the poor "saints" in Jerusalem.

Acts 15: 1 and 5 relate that a number of followers of Jesus from Judea came to Antioch and taught that believers had to be

6. VIEWS OF THE ORIGINAL CHRISTIANS REGARDING JESUS

circumcised, according to the Law of Moses. This affirms that these Jewish followers of Jesus adhered to all the Old Testament laws and continued to live as Jews. They, no doubt, quoted Jesus who reportedly taught:

> "Whoever then goes against the smallest of these laws, teaching men to do the same, will be named least in the kingdom of heaven; but he who keeps the laws, teaching others to keep them, will be named great in the kingdom of heaven" (Matt 5: 19).

They also found support in these words of Jesus:

> "But it is easier for heaven and earth to pass away, than for one tiny stroke of a pen in the law to fall" (Luke 16: 17).

They did not see themselves as belonging to a new religion and most probably came to investigate Paul's doctrines in Antioch, which seemed to differ from Jesus' teachings. We read that Paul and Barnabas disagreed with these Jewish followers of Jesus and that the congregation in Antioch resolved to send Paul, Barnabas and others to Jerusalem to settle the issue. The people who came from Judea to Antioch must have known Jesus personally while he was still alive, while Paul and Barnabas – who thought that these people taught a heresy – never knew Jesus personally.

Paul tells his readers in Gal 2: 11–21 that he and Peter clashed publicly in Antioch about the obligation of followers of Jesus to live according to the Old Testament laws. This must be an indication that Peter was one of those who came to Antioch to investigate Paul's teachings as recorded in Acts 15: 1. That means that the Apostle Peter didn't regard himself as a Christian – he was simply a Jewish follower of Jesus, a Nazorean.

6. VIEWS OF THE ORIGINAL CHRISTIANS REGARDING JESUS

Paul also had a meeting with James, brother of Jesus and leader of the movement in Jerusalem, and the elders during his last visit to that city before his arrest. James told Paul that "many thousands there are among the Jews of those who have believed, and they are all zealous for the law" (Acts 21: 20). In other words: the Jewish followers of Jesus in Judea continued to live as Jews and they merely formed an influential sect or group within the Jewish religious community.

James also informed Paul that these followers of Jesus could not agree with his teachings since "you teach all the Jews who are among the Gentiles to forsake Moses, telling them not to circumcise their children neither to walk after the customs" (Acts 21: 21). Paul was then forced to undergo the Jewish purifying rites before he could be allowed to enter the temple and bring sacrifices according to the laws of Moses (Acts 21: 24–26). The fact that Paul succumbed to these requirements is an indication that he realized that James was an influential person and that he could not afford to lose his sympathy and support – although he must have thought that these ceremonies were unnecessary and that they clashed with his view that Christ has fulfilled and abolished the obligations of the Jewish Law (Gal 3: 13).

At the outbreak of the Jewish war of AD 66–70, a number of these Jewish followers of Jesus fled to Pella on the eastern side of the Jordan and to Syria, where they continued to practice their brand of Jewish Christianity. They also spread to Egypt and Asia Minor.

Christian theologians of the second century AD and afterwards regarded them as heretics since they denied the virgin birth and divinity of Christ.[147] Justin Martyr, the Christian apologist of the second century AD, for instance, was aware of "Christians"

---

[147] Jewish Encyclopaedia, "Ebionites"; Encyclopaedia Britannica, "Ebionite"; Eusebius: Liber III/V/3 & XXVII/5–6.

6. VIEWS OF THE ORIGINAL CHRISTIANS REGARDING JESUS

holding the view that Jesus was nothing but an ordinary man. In his Dialogue with Trypho he places the following words in the mouth of his opponent Trypho:

> "Those who affirm him [Jesus] to have been a man, and to have been anointed by election, and then to have become Christ, appear to me to speak more plausibly than you who hold those opinions which you express. For we all expect that Christ will be a man [born] of men..."[148]

Irenaeus, another theologian of the second century AD, described the Ebionites in the following words:

> "Those who are called Ebionites agree that the world was made by God; but their opinions with respect to the Lord are similar to those of Cerinthus and Carpocrates. They use the Gospel according to Matthew only, and repudiate the Apostle Paul, maintaining that he was an apostate from the law. As to the prophetical writings, they endeavor to expound them in a somewhat singular manner: they practice circumcision, persevere in the observance of those customs which are enjoined by the law, and are so Judaic in their style of life, that they even adore Jerusalem as if it were the house of God."[149]

Several scholars agree that the early Jewish followers of Jesus in Judea and Galilee were indeed none other than the Ebionites (and the Nazoreans) who denied the virgin birth of Jesus and his divine nature. Michael Goulder concluded that this stance was "was the

---

[148] Justin Martyr, *Dialogue with Trypho*, ch 49)
[149] Irenaeus, *Adversus Haereses*, Liber I/XXVI/2.

6. VIEWS OF THE ORIGINAL CHRISTIANS REGARDING JESUS

creed of the Jerusalem Church from early times."[150] Gerd Lüdemann thought that "the group of Ebionites should be seen as an offshoot of the Jerusalem community."[151] According to Robert Eisenman, the first leader of the Ebionites was none other than James, the brother of Jesus.[152] John Painter saw a "connection between early Jerusalem Christianity (the Hebrews) and the later Ebionites."[153]

That the Ebionites (and Nazoreans) were opposed to Paul and his teaching, is no surprise. During Paul's last visit to Jerusalem and the temple, some Jews from Asia assaulted him because they said: "Men of Israel, help! This is the man who teaches all men everywhere against the people, and the law, and this place" (Acts 21: 27–28).

It is not unreasonable to surmise that Q had its origin amongst these Ebionites while they still resided in and around Judea. Their version of the Gospel according to Matthew could have been none other than Q.

Kinzig remarks: "[T]hey appear to have read the Gospel of Matthew in an archaic 'Hebrew,' i.e., probably Aramaic version."[154] He elaborates that "there was in principle only one Aramaic gospel, called 'according to the Hebrews,' which was used by the Nazoraeans and other groups. This gospel was written at around 100 C.E. and was considered the Ur-Matthäus."[155]

Due to the fact that the Ebionites and Nazoreans were the Jewish followers of Jesus and their direct descendants in Jerusalem and Judea, one can expect that they retained more authentic

---

[150] Goulder, *St. Paul versus St. Peter*, 134.
[151] Lüdemann, *Heretics*, 52.
[152] Eisenman, *James*, 154–56.
[153] Painter, *Just James*, 229.
[154] Kinzig, "The Nazoreans", 472.
[155] Kinzig, "The Nazoreans", 473.

6. VIEWS OF THE ORIGINAL CHRISTIANS REGARDING JESUS

memories of Jesus than Christians elsewhere who depended upon the four gospels and the writings of Paul for information regarding Jesus. In other words: the view of the Ebionites and Nazoreans that Jesus was an ordinary mortal, that he was the son of Joseph and Mary and not a divine figure must be regarded as definitely more convincing and authoritative than the views of other Christians who worshipped him as the eternal and divine Son of God, the equal of God the Father.

The Letters of James and Jude
The letters of James and Jude (Judas), two short documents contained in the New Testament, were very probably written by leaders of the early Jewish "Christian" congregation in Jerusalem. They can, therefore, be regarded as the earliest records of the Ebionite movement, apart from Q.

Amongst experts, there is agreement that the letter of James originated in a Jewish "Christian" community. It is, after all, addressed "to the twelve tribes which are in the Dispersion" (Jas 1: 1) – by which the Jewish followers of Jesus must have been meant. In Jas 2: 2 mention is made of an "assembly" where the word "synagogue" (Greek: συναγωγή – *synagoge*) is actually used. There are many allusions to the Old Testament.

There is no agreement as to who the author was and when it was written. Some experts date it late in the first century AD when James, the brother of Jesus and leader of the Ebionites in Jerusalem, was already deceased. According to Josephus, he was killed in AD 62.

There are also those who believe that the author was, in fact, James, the brother of Jesus. In this letter, no mention is made of the destruction of the temple and hostility of the Jews towards the followers of Jesus. The social situation also seems to mirror the period before the destruction of Jerusalem in AD 70 when a number

6. VIEWS OF THE ORIGINAL CHRISTIANS REGARDING JESUS

of rich landowners exploited the poor (Jas 5: 1–6). A possible date for the letter may be during the forties or fifties of the first century – at most two decades after the death of Jesus and before or contemporary with the letters of Paul.

It is to be remarked that more than one passage in this letter, which deals mainly with ethical issues, refers to poverty and riches – which tallies with the idea that it originated with the Ebionites, the poor Jewish followers of Jesus.[156] For instance, James wrote: "Didn't God choose those who are poor in this world to be rich in faith, and heirs of the kingdom which he promised to those who love him?" (Jas 2: 5.

This aversion of wealth and opulence was also to be found with the Essenes or Nazoreans, who formed the core of the Jesus Movement – as pointed out previously.

Jesus is only mentioned twice in this letter. In Jas 1: 1 the author identifies himself as "James, a servant of God and of the Lord Jesus Christ". In Jas 2:1 he writes: "My brothers, don't hold the faith of our Lord Jesus Christ, [the Lord] of glory, with respect of persons."

The word for "Lord" in Greek is κύριος (*kyrios*), a word often used in the New Testament for The Lord (God). Its literal meaning is actually a title of honor expressive of respect and reverence, with which servants greeted their masters. Thiede and D'Ancona note: "The word 'Lord', *kyrios,* for instance, could be applied to persons far removed from the holy Trinity...."[157]

If Jesus Christ, the Messiah, is named "Lord", it does not necessarily mean that he is regarded as a divine being; it may simply mean that he was held in high regard as a master or teacher. The

---

[156] Encyclopaedia Britannica, "James, The letter of"; Encyclopaedia Britannica, "Biblical Literature"; Gaum, *Kernensiklopedie,* 510–11.
[157] Thiede and D'Ancona, *The Jesus Papyrus,* 162.

6. VIEWS OF THE ORIGINAL CHRISTIANS REGARDING JESUS

translation in Jas 2: 1 of "[the Lord] of glory" is an indication that the word "Lord" does not occur in the original, but was inserted by the translators for the sake of clarity. The expression may also be translated as "our master Jesus Christ who is to be regarded as honorable (or: with a good reputation)."

When identifies himself as "James, a servant of God and of the Lord Jesus Christ" (Ἰάκωβος θεοῦ καὶ κυρίου Ἰησοῦ Ξριστοῦ δοῦλος – *Iakobous theou kai kuriou Iesou Christou doulos*), it is clear that he regards God and the Lord Jesus Christ as two separate persons, beings or entities. He separates the two with the word "and". If he had regarded Jesus to be God Himself, he would not have used the word "and" as he did.

When Jas 2: 1 mentions "the faith of our Lord Jesus Christ" it cannot mean faith *in* Jesus Christ – it can only point to the teachings of Jesus.

The expectation of the Ebionites that Jesus would return soon is repeated in James: "You also be patient. Establish your hearts, for the coming of the Lord is at hand" (Jas 5: 8).

When all these considerations are taken into regard, it is very reasonable to accept that the letter of James was written by Jesus' brother and that it reflects the ideas of the Ebionites or Nazoreans who lived according to the Law of Moses and did not regard Jesus as divine, but expected his return.

Although the letter of Jude (Judas) mentions "Jude, a servant of Jesus Christ, and brother of James" as author, most experts believe that the author is actually anonymous and that the letter was written towards the end of the first century. Should the author really have been Jude, a brother of James, then he also would have been a brother of Jesus (Mark 6: 3). The word "brother" may also mean "relative" or even "nephew" – in which case the author could have

6. VIEWS OF THE ORIGINAL CHRISTIANS REGARDING JESUS

been the Judas who succeeded James and Symeon as leader of die Jerusalem congregation.[158]

According to some, the allusion to "the apostles of our Lord Jesus Christ" in verse 17 may be an indication of a late date.[159] This does not seem very convincing; it may also mean that Jude reminds his readers of what the apostles said, something they still could remember.

The letter also seems to have originated in a Jewish "Christian" setting. The letter warns against licentious heretics who will be judged by God and to prove this, the Old Testament is frequently quoted.

Jesus Christ is mentioned five times:

- The author describes himself as "a servant of Jesus Christ" (vs 1).
- Verse 1 also informs us that this letter is addressed to "those who are called, sanctified by God the Father, and kept for Jesus Christ".
- The main thrust of the letter is against heretics who are "denying our only Master, God, and Lord, Jesus Christ" (vs 4). The word "God" in this verse does not appear in the original Greek. Jesus is described as a master (Greek: δεσπότης – *despotes*, despot or master).
- Mention was already made to "the apostles of our Lord Jesus Christ" in verse 17.
- The benediction at the end of the letter reads: "To the only God our Savior, through Jesus Christ our Lord, let us give

---

[158] Eusebius, Liber III/XXXII/5
[159] Gaum, *Kernensiklopedie,* 548–49; Encyclopaedia Britannica, "Jude, Letter of"; Encyclopaedia Britannica, "Biblical Literature".

6. VIEWS OF THE ORIGINAL CHRISTIANS REGARDING JESUS

> glory and honor and authority and power, before all time and now and for ever."

Jude, therefore, thinks of Jesus Christ as a messiah and a master to whose flock the believers belong and to whom they must be loyal. Jesus is not mentioned as a savior – that appellation is reserved for God only. It does seem very probable that the author of this letter did not regard Jesus as a divine or supernatural being.

Jude provided very little information regarding the views of the heretics he warned against. We are told that they were guilty of sexual malpractices, that they defiled the communal meals and that they "deny" Jesus Christ. This denial has traditionally been interpreted as meaning that these heretics refused to acknowledge that Jesus Christ was the Son of God and the savior of mankind. But this interpretation is not necessarily supported by the text. If this letter really originated within Ebionite circles, which regarded Paul as a heretic, then this denial of Jesus Christ may also mean that these heretics denied that he was merely a human being.

It is known from various warnings in the letters of Paul that Christians in gentile communities often made themselves guilty of immorality, that they behaved badly during communal meals and that they even participated in pagan ceremonies – which would have horrified any Jew, including Jesus' Jewish followers (1 Cor 5; 1 Cor 11: 27–34; 2 Cor 12: 21; Eph 5: 3, 18; 1 Thess 4: 3; Rev 2: 20). The heretics, against whom Jude warns his readers, may well have been those gentile Christians who believed that Jesus Christ is God made flesh, but who also lived immorally.

From the preceding it is clear, or at least highly probable, that the early Jewish followers of Jesus, where the letters of James and Jude originated, did not regard Jesus as anything but an ordinary mortal human being.

6. VIEWS OF THE ORIGINAL CHRISTIANS REGARDING JESUS

The Didache

A document known as the "Didache" and whose full translated title is "The Teaching of the Lord through the Twelve Apostles" (Διδαχὴ Κυρίου διὰ τῶν δώδεκα ἀποστόλων – *Didache Kuriou dia ton dodeka apostolon*), surfaced only in 1873 and immediately caused a stir since it proved to be the oldest Christian document not contained in the New Testament.

There is uncertainty regarding its date. Some authorities place it in the early second century AD,[160] while experts such as Luschnig and Luschnig found that at least certain parts were written during the forties and fifties of the first century AD – contemporary with the letters of Paul.[161]

Luschnig and Luschnig describe it as "a manual of early church discipline and church practices probably from the church in Syria, near Antioch, where the new believers were first called 'Christians.'" The author's name is unknown and the title is only a description of its contents. It is clear, though, that the author (or editor), who addresses his readers as "my children", was a Jewish believer who knew the Old Testament well, although he often quoted sayings of Jesus known from oral traditions – which agree with the reports of Jesus' teachings in the gospels.[162]

The author could have known some of the apostles of Jesus, who passed on Jesus' teachings to his other followers – hence the title of the document.[163]

The following topics are dealt with in the Didache:

- The two ways: the way of life and the way of death;
- Baptism;

---

[160] Encylopaedia Britannica, "Didache".
[161] Luschnig and Luschnig, *The Teaching of the Twelve*, 1.
[162] Luschnig and Luschnig, *The Teaching of the Twelve*, 1–3.
[163] Luschnig and Luschnig, *The Teaching of the Twelve*, 12–13.

6. VIEWS OF THE ORIGINAL CHRISTIANS REGARDING JESUS

- Fasting and prayer;
- The Eucharist and Eucharist prayer;
- Wandering teachers;
- Prophets, true and false;
- Christian wayfarers and immigrants;
- Payment of prophets and teachers;
- Sunday worship in the community;
- Choosing bishops and deacons from the community; and
- The last days.

The "way of life" according to the Didache differs substantially from the message of salvation given in Paul's epistles and the gospels. The well-known John 3: 16 states:

> "For God so loved the world, that he gave his one and only Son, that whoever believes in him should not perish, but have eternal life."

Nothing of this sort is to be found in the Didache. The only way to please God and find the way of life is as follows:

> "The way of life is this: 'First, you shalt love the God who made thee, secondly, thy neighbor as thyself; and whatsoever thou wouldst not have done to thyself, do not thou to another'" (Did 1: 2).

There is nothing to suggest that one should put one's trust in Jesus Christ to be saved, as Christians are made to believe in Paul's letters and the gospels.

The way in which Jesus is treated in this document is also interesting. He is four times referred to as "Jesus thy child/son" – that is, God's child or son (Did 9: 2; 9: 3; 10:2; 10: 3). This does not mean that Jesus is regarded as the only Son of God and of the same

6. VIEWS OF THE ORIGINAL CHRISTIANS REGARDING JESUS

substance as God, for we also read of "David thy child/son" (Did 9: 2). When Jesus and David are both called sons of God it is an expression to emphasize their royal status as Israelite kings. The title "Christ" is used twice, once in conjunction with the name Jesus. That may only mean that Jesus was regarded as a messiah, an anointed of God.

The prayers to be said at the Eucharist (Did 9 and 10) deviate markedly from what would have been expected from a Christian celebration of the Eucharist. Jesus' death on the cross is nowhere mentioned.

Converts are, though, to be baptized in "the Name of the Father and of the Son and of the Holy Ghost" in accordance with Matt 28: 19 (Did 7: 1, 3). It is possible that this is a later addition.

Luschnig and Luschnig conclude: "But to the earliest one or two generations of followers of Jesus, his religion seemed not to be different from Judaism but, rather, reformed and perfected Judaism."[164] This reformed Judaism – which may be equated with Ebionism – had no place for a deified Christ. Jesus is portrayed in the Didache merely as a wise teacher, not the eternal divine Son of God.

The author(s) of the Didache shared the antipathy of the Essenes and Ebionites towards rich people. In Did 5: 2 we are told that the "Way of Death" is followed by all sorts of sinners, including "lovers of vanity, following after reward, unmerciful to the poor, not working for him who is oppressed with toil, without knowledge of him who made them, murderers of children, corrupters of God's creatures, turning away the needy, oppressing the distressed, advocates of the rich, unjust judges of the poor..."

That these early followers of Jesus did not see themselves as anything but Jews is borne out by the archaeological record.

---

[164] Luschnig and Luschnig, *The Teaching of the Twelve*, 4.

6. VIEWS OF THE ORIGINAL CHRISTIANS REGARDING JESUS

Excavations of sites in Judea and Galilee dating from the first century AD demonstrate that no site can be regarded as specific Christian. Meyers and Chancey note: "The material culture of the earliest followers of Jesus is extremely difficult to identify, precisely because it was largely indistinguishable from that of other Jews."[165]

The Fate of the Ebionites

The Ebionites, the Jewish followers of Jesus, faded from history. Two factors caused their demise:

- The success of the mission of the apostle Paul who propagated a new religion, distinct from the Jewish religion; and
- The aftermath of the Jewish War against the Romans.

Paul's contribution will be discussed later.

The outcome of the Jewish War of AD 66–70 amounted to a huge catastrophe for all Jews throughout the Roman Empire – not only for those who were living in Judea and Galilee. All Jews from whatever religious party or sect were subjected to harsh discrimination and humiliation.

After Jerusalem was destroyed and many Jews were crucified or enslaved, Emperor Vespasian minted coins on which his victory was commemorated. On the reverse side, Judea was pictured as a chained woman, guarded by an armed soldier. The inscription read: IVDEA CAPTA (Judea captured). These coins were coined for 25 years, long after the death of Vespasian, by his sons Titus and Domitian who succeed him.[166] Every inhabitant of the Roman Empire was constantly reminded of the humiliating defeat of the

---

[165] Meyers and Chancey, *Alexander to Constatine*, 177.
[166] Ngo, "Judea Capta Coin".

6. VIEWS OF THE ORIGINAL CHRISTIANS REGARDING JESUS

Jews whenever he looked at one of these coins, which was meant to serve as a warning that it was futile to challenge the military might of Rome.

IVDEA CAPTA coin minted by Emperor Vespasian to celebrate the defeat of the Jews

Domitian imposed a tax on all Jews and Christians – the difference between these two religions was unclear to outsiders at that time – to punish them for the revolt of AD 66–70 at an amount equivalent to the temple tax that Jews had to pay before the destruction of the temple. This tax, called the *Fiscus Iudaicus*, went for the upkeep of the temple of Jupiter Capitolinus in Rome. Those who tried to dodge this tax had their property confiscated. Needless to say, this tax caused much resentment and was partly abolished by his successor, Nerva.[167] This discrimination against the Jewish followers of Jesus would not have made this movement attractive to potential converts.

It has already been shown that the four gospels contain a pronounced anti-Semitic flavor in order to present Christianity in as favorable a light as possible to the Roman world. It was in the interest of gentile Christians to demonstrate that their religion differed from the Jewish religion and that it was a fit religion for Greeks and Romans.

---

[167] Elkins, "Roman Emperor Nerva's Reform".

6. VIEWS OF THE ORIGINAL CHRISTIANS REGARDING JESUS

The Jewish followers of Jesus suffered just as much as other Jews. They were regarded as heretics by Christians because they did not subscribe to the notion that Jesus Christ was a divine personage, God in human form. Other Jews most probably shunned them due to the fact that there were similarities between them and the Christian movement. The Jews could also not forget that the Jewish followers of Jesus, for the most part, refused to take part in the Jewish War and they were, therefore, regarded as turncoats or traitors.

It is, therefore, hardly a surprise that the movement of the Ebionites lost momentum and disappeared sometime during the fourth century AD.[168]

---

[168] Encyclopaedia Britannica, "Ebionite".

CHAPTER 7

PAUL'S VISIONS AND REVELATIONS

A Divine Being

The epistles of Paul, Peter and John, the four gospels, the book of Acts, the letter to the Hebrews and the book of Revelation all proclaim the belief that Jesus Christ was *the* Messiah, the only-begotten Son of God, a human being but also God incarnate.

Two passages from Paul, who wrote his letters during the fifties of the first century, can be quoted in this regard:

> "Let this mind be in you which was in Christ Jesus, to whom, though himself in the form of God, it did not seem that to take for oneself was to be like God; but he made himself as nothing, taking the form of a servant, being made like men; and being seen in form as a man, he took the lowest place, and let himself be put to death, even the death of the cross. For this reason God has put him in the highest place and has given to him the name which is greater than every name; so that at the name of Jesus every knee may be bent, of those in heaven and those on earth and those in the underworld, and that every tongue may give witness that Jesus Christ is Lord, to the glory of God the Father" (Phil 2: 5–11).

This passage comes from a hymn known to his readers, which Paul quotes in this letter. It is clear that he supported the idea that Jesus Christ was "in the form of God" and "like God", and also that everybody ought to worship him.

In Col 1: 15–17 we read:

7. PAUL'S VIVIONS AND REVELATIONS

> "[Christ] who is the image of the invisible God, the firstborn of all creation. For in him were all things created, in the heavens and on the earth, things visible and things invisible, whether thrones or dominions or principalities or powers; all things have been created through him, and to him. He is before all things, and in him all things are held together."

These words are also part of an old hymn and Paul quotes them to prove that Christ "is the image of the invisible God", that he is eternal, that he is the principle through which creation was called into being and that he is the highest authority in all of creation.

Paul never knew Jesus when he was alive. Paul initially tried to suppress the Christian movement but then he received visions or revelations, which convinced him that he must, henceforth, serve Christ (1 Cor 15: 8; 2 Cor 12: 1–10; Gal 1: 11 – 2: 14).

It is clear that the gospels repeated what Paul taught regarding the divinity of Jesus Christ. Karen Armstrong declares:

> "Writing in the fifties CE, Paul is the earliest extant Christian author and his teachings influenced the accounts of Jesus' life in the Gospels of Mark, Matthew and Luke (known as the Synoptics), written in the seventies and eighties." [169]

In the book of Revelation, Jesus Christ is portrayed as the heavenly judge who will condemn sinners to hell and allow the faithful to enter heaven (Rev 20–22).

Paul's Thorn in the Flesh

How did it come that Paul had these visions and revelations? This will become clearer when one investigates the reports in his letters

---

[169] Armstrong, *Fields of Blood,* 126.

7. PAUL'S VIVIONS AND REVELATIONS

regarding his experiences. A key passage in this regard is 2 Cor 12: 1–7 –

> "It is doubtless not profitable for me to boast. I will come to visions and revelations of the Lord. I know a man in Christ, fourteen years ago (whether in the body, I don`t know, or whether out of the body, I don`t know; God knows), such a one caught up into the third heaven. I know such a man (whether in the body, or apart from the body, I don`t know; God knows), how he was caught up into Paradise, and heard unspeakable words, which it is not lawful for a man to utter. On behalf of such a one I will boast, but on my own behalf I will not boast, except in my weaknesses. (. . .) By reason of the exceeding greatness of the revelations, that I should not be exalted excessively, there was given to me a thorn in the flesh, a messenger of Satan to buffet me, that I should not be exalted excessively."

The following relevant aspects regarding this passage have to be pointed out:

- Although Paul employs the third person singular, it is clear that he refers to himself;
- He had experienced visions and revelations (plural) during which he heard voices uttering unspeakable words;
- He experienced Paradise and was caught up to the third heaven (the heaven above the heaven of clouds and the starry heaven, *i.e.,* die dwelling place of God and the angels); and
- He is not certain whether he had these experiences while in or out of his body.

What exactly was this "thorn in the flesh"? Various possibilities were given of which the most probable will be explored further on.

7. PAUL'S VIVIONS AND REVELATIONS

The word for "thorn" that Paul uses is σκόλοψ (*skolops*). It means "a pointed piece of wood, a pale, a sharp stake, splinter". It must, therefore, have been something very painful or uncomfortable.

The passage quoted above is not the only one in which he alludes to his visions and revelations. In numerous passages, such as Acts 16:9, 18:9 and 22: 17–21, 1 Cor 4: 1, 1 Cor 9: 1, 1 Cor 15: 3–8, 2 Cor 5: 16, 2 Cor 12: 12, Gal 1: 11–16, Eph 3: 2–3, and 1 Thess. 2: 4, we read of visions which Paul said he had had, mostly of the risen and glorified Christ, through which the "mysteries" of the gospel were revealed to him.

When reading these passages, one cannot but be reminded of the three accounts of Paul's conversion on the road to Damascus given in Acts 9: 3–19, 22: 6–16 and 26: 12–20. The following points may be made regarding these descriptions, while keeping in mind that the author of Acts wrote his history several decades after the event and could have become confused regarding certain details. After all, the accounts of Paul's conversion in Acts differ markedly from his own rendering of the event in Galatians 1.[170]

- Paul travelled to Damascus and suddenly saw a bright light, which his travelling companions couldn't see;
- He fell to the earth;
- He heard a voice; his companions also heard the voice but could not understand the words;
- The voice told him that it was Jesus, whose followers he had persecuted;
- He was blinded and had to be led by the hand by his companions the rest of the way;
- He rarely moved for three days, not even eating and drinking;

---

[170] Rylaarsdam et al., "Biblical Literature".

7. PAUL'S VIVIONS AND REVELATIONS

- He recovered his eyesight after three days through the ministrations of Ananias, a local Christian, who also baptized him; and
- The whole experience must have been traumatic for Paul.

Paul's mode of travel to Damascus is not mentioned. Many artistic renderings of the event depict him as falling from a horse. That seems unlikely. He and his companions probably travelled on foot and that explains why he had to be led by hand by his companions when he became blind.

The fact that Paul had a fall and became temporarily sightless, as well as the fact that he rarely moved during the following three days, may lead to the conclusion that a neurological condition, such as a serious concussion, may have occurred.

It has to be added that there is the distinct possibility that Paul suffered from bad eyesight, which could, perhaps, have been the result of his experience on the road to Damascus. He regularly used a secretary to whom he dictated his letters and he only signed off his letters with his own hand in large letters (Rom 16: 22; 1 Cor 16: 21; Gal 6: 11; 2 Thess 3: 17). Acts 23: 2–5 describes an episode where Paul insulted the retired high priest, Annas, and afterwards apologized because he didn't recognize him – perhaps due to his faulty eyesight.

7. PAUL'S VIVIONS AND REVELATIONS

Caravaggio: Conversion of St Paul (1601)

Paul also seems to have suffered a lot physically. We read in the following texts of the pain, weaknesses, frailty and persecutions he endured: 2 Cor 4: 7–9, 2 Cor 4: 16–18, 2 Cor 12:10, 2 Cor 13: 4 and Gal 4: 13–14.

Hallucinations

The conventional view is that Paul's various visions of Christ must have been supernatural events. There is, however, also a real possibility that he experienced hallucinations. When one submits that so-called supernatural revelations and visions are by their very nature subjective and, therefore, impossible to be verified independently, then one also has to accept that they cannot be anything but hallucinations or delusions.

7. PAUL'S VIVIONS AND REVELATIONS

The fifth edition (2013) of the Diagnostic and Statistical Manual of Mental Disorders of the American Psychiatric Association (DSM-5) provides the following description of *hallucinations*:

> "Hallucinations are perception-like experiences that occur without an external stimulus. They are vivid and clear, with the full force and impact of normal perceptions, and not under voluntary control. They may occur in any sensory modality, but auditory hallucinations are the most common in schizophrenia and related disorders. Auditory hallucinations are usually experienced as voices, whether familiar or unfamiliar, that are perceived as distinct from the individual's own thoughts."[171]

Investigators, such as the late neurologist Prof Oliver Sacks of the New York University Medical School, have noted that hallucinations often have religious overtones for those who experience them. These people may be convinced that they experienced a profound spiritual awakening or an encounter with God, Jesus, another divine being, deceased loved ones or other spiritual beings. Sacks points out that Joan of Arc, who had seizures, was convinced that God called her to become a religious and military leader in France in medieval times.[172]

Hallucinations may be caused by a variety of factors:

- Psychedelic drugs;
- A near-death-experience or out-of-the-body experience;
- Psychosis, such as schizophrenia;

---

[171] APA, *DSM-5*, 87.
[172] Sacks, *Hallucinations*; O'Callaghan, "Oliver Sacks Wants to Destigmatize Hallucinations".

7. PAUL'S VIVIONS AND REVELATIONS

- An attack of migraine;
- Epilepsy;
- Stroke;
- Charles Bonnet Syndrome;
- Delirium tremens;
- Sensory deprivation;
- Sensory defects;
- Loss of sleep;
- Hypnosis and trance states; or
- Traumatic brain injuries and brain tumors.[173]

The most important of these possibilities will be discussed below:

Psychedelic Drugs

There is no indication in the Bible that Paul ever used or abused drugs. Hancock is convinced, though, that Paul's visions were drug-induced, just as was the case with many other religious visionaries.[174] Whether that really happened, is impossible to determine today.

It is known, however, that opium and cannabis leaves (chewed or boiled in a tea) were used as medicine and pain-killers throughout the ancient Middle East[175] and the possibility exists that Paul could have used these substances to counter pain, possibly migraine or other ailments. After all, he endured many painful and harrowing experiences. He remembers:

> "Five times from the Jews I received forty stripes minus one. Three times I was beaten with rods. Once I was stoned. Three

---

[173] Wallis, "What do Hallucinations Tell"; West, "Hallucinations".
[174] Hancock, *Supernatural,* 496–97.
[175] Medical Brief, 18.02.2015.

7. PAUL'S VIVIONS AND REVELATIONS

times I suffered ship-wreck. I have been a night and a day in the deep" (2 Cor 11: 24–25).

It is, therefore, not impossible that Paul used the above-mentioned pain-killers. Opium, which is the dried juice of unripe poppy seedpods, originated either in Asia Minor or Cyprus during the Bronze Age and was still widely in use during Paul's day. Opium contains, amongst others, the pain-killers morphine and codeine.[176] Drugs derived from opium and called opioids are today still being used as potent analgesics. Migraine is often treated with morphine. Opioids, like morphine and codeine, may cause euphoria.[177]

An overdose of opioids often causes confusion, sleepiness, slurred speech, unconsciousness, slow breathing, seizures, drowsiness, dizziness and hallucinations. These drugs are addictive and cessation after prolonged use cause unpleasant withdrawal symptoms, including anxiety, depression, cramps, painful limbs, nausea and fever.[178]

Cannabis – also known as marijuana – is native to India, but was known throughout the ancient Near East as medicine. As a pain-killer, it causes euphoria. An overdose may lead to hallucinations, anxiety, depression, paranoid reactions or even psychosis.[179] Withdrawal symptoms after prolonged use can lead to irritability, anger and insomnia.[180]

It is well-known that psychedelic drugs were used in religious rituals in Mediterranean countries during antiquity. The

---

[176] Stein, "Psychedelics"; Encyclopaedia Britannica, "Opium".
[177] Clark et al., *Pharmacology*, 170, 176, 555.
[178] Holford, *How to Quit Without Feeling S**t*, 345.
[179] Encyclopaedia Britannica, "Marijuana"; Keyser, "Drug Trade".
[180] Holford, *How to Quit Without Feeling S**t*, 334.

7. PAUL'S VIVIONS AND REVELATIONS

drug-induced trances and hallucinations caused altered states of consciousness, ecstasy, mania and unity with a deity.[181]

One may wonder whether Paul's visions of the risen Christ could have been induced by some drug and whether his "thorn in the flesh" could have been the symptoms of an overdose or a case of withdrawal when he no longer had a supply of these drugs.

John of Patmos, the author of the book of Revelation, reported: "I was in the Spirit on the Lord's day, and I heard behind me a loud voice, as of a trumpet" (Rev 1: 10). He also mentions in Rev 4: 2; 17: 3 and 21: 10 that he was, on occasion, "in the Spirit" when he had certain visions. One cannot but wonder whether this "Spirit" was not some or other drug that made him hear voices and see a number of angels. monsters and beasts in the sky.

Near-Death Experience or Out-of-the-Body Experience

People undergoing a near-death experience (NDE) or an out-of-body experience (OBE) usually have visions of a perceived afterlife. After the event, they report tunnel vision, a bright light at the end of the tunnel, euphoria and meetings with other-worldly beings, usually interpreted as God, Jesus, another deity, angels and/or deceased loved ones. During this type of event, people mostly experience a loss of consciousness and a feeling of weightlessness.

Since Dr Raymond Moody first described this phenomenon in 1975, much research has been done. A NDE or OBE can be induced by electrical stimulation of certain parts of the brain or by anoxia, the lack of oxygen. The feeling of euphoria can be attributed to the release of the neurotransmitters (brain chemicals) dopamine, serotonin and endorphins. It has been found that Buddhist monks and Franciscan nuns, who are able to go into a deep state of meditation, trance and self-hypnosis, are also able to induce an

---

[181] Encyclopaedia Britannica, "Drug cult".

7. PAUL'S VIVIONS AND REVELATIONS

OBE, which they explain as a religious ecstatic condition. Damage to parts of the parietal lobe in the brain or a traumatic experience, such as a near-fatal heart attack, can also have this effect.[182]

It will be shown in a later paragraph that the possibility of mild traumatic brain damage in Paul on the Damascus Road cannot be ruled out. His harrowing experiences of assaults, torture and shipwreck, while spending long hours in the water (2 Cor 11: 24–25), may also have contributed to a NDE or OBE's in his case. That might explain his encounters with the risen Christ. The fact that he states in 2 Cor 12: 1–5 that he cannot say whether he experienced the third heaven and Paradise in or out of the body suggests that his experience on the Damascus Road, where he saw a bright light, could have been a NDE or an OBE.

Temporal Lobe Epilepsy

Landsborough, a neurologist, presented a convincing case that Paul's thorn in the flesh could have been left temporal lobe epilepsy.[183] In many cases, epilepsy is an inherited condition, but it may also be caused by trauma, infection, fever, tumors or toxins. It is the result of an abnormal firing of neurons in one region of the brain, spreading to other parts. Many neurons lose their regular rhythm and switch to a rapid rhythm, due to the overproduction of Sestrin-3. The result is a seizure or a convulsion (*ictus*).[184]

Seizures are often preceded by an aura, a sensation that an attack is imminent. A so-called grand mal seizure results in a loss of consciousness, temporary paralysis and loss of control over the muscles. The loss of consciousness may be for only a few seconds

---

[182] Shermer, *The Believing Bain*, 152–55; Stenger, *The New Atheism*, 182.
[183] Landsborough, "St Paul and Temporal Lobe Epilepsy".
[184] Kolb and Wishaw, *Fundamentals of Human Neuropsychology*, 757–58; University of Bonn, "Dragnet for Epilepsy Genes."

7. PAUL'S VIVIONS AND REVELATIONS

or much longer. A petit mal seizure is not so severe and consists mainly of a shut-down of consciousness for a few seconds. The intervals between attacks may be minutes, hours, days or months.[185]

Epilepsy may be due to abnormalities in the occipital lobe at the back of the head where the visual centers of the brain are located. This may result in visual hallucinations containing people and other aspects of reality. Partial blindness may accompany attacks.[186]

Abnormalities in the temporal lobes of the brain – just behind the eyes – are responsible for most cases of epilepsy.[187] If the abnormalities are centered in the speech centers within the left temporal lobe and the underlying limbic system, the attacks may be accompanied by auditory and/or visual hallucinations, which may be interpreted by the sufferer as having spiritual or religious significance.[188]

Paul's repeated visions, his temporary blindness and his visual problems do seem to be the result of left temporal lobe epileptic seizures. Since this disease was known in antiquity as the "sacred disease", during which various gods – especially *Selene* (Σελήνη), the moon goddess – supposedly spoke to the sufferer, it may account for Paul's success with Gentile audiences who must have concluded that he was in direct contact with his God while experiencing a fit.[189]

---

[185] Kolb and Wishaw, *Fundamentals of Human Neuropsychology,* 757–58; Aminoff, *Encyclopaedia of the Neurological Sciences,* 250–55.
[186] NYU Langone Comprehensive Epilepsy Center, "Occipital Lobe Epilepsy".
[187] Landsborough, "St Paul and Temporal Lobe Epilepsy", 663.
[188] Hoffman et al. "Transcranial Magnetic Stimulation", 55; Elliot et al., "Delusions"; Korsness et al. "An fMRI Study", 610, 616.
[189] Jewish Encyclopaedia, "Epilepsy"; Riggs and Riggs, "Epilepsy's Role", 452; Magiorkinis et al., 2012: 132; See Matt 17:15 where the

7. PAUL'S VIVIONS AND REVELATIONS

Recent trials have confirmed that epilepsy may be treated and alleviated with cannabidiol, an extract of the cannabis plant (Fiore, 2016). There is a possibility that Paul might have found that cannabis relieved his epileptic fits, if his "thorn in the flesh" was indeed epilepsy. His hallucinations may, therefore, have been a combination of epilepsy and the use of cannabis.

Mild Traumatic Brain Injury
A possibility not considered by any other investigator – as far as can be ascertained – is that Paul may have suffered from the after-effects of a concussion and mild traumatic brain injury.

All three accounts of Paul's conversion in Acts mention that he fell to the ground when he saw a bright light. The seriousness of this fall is not mentioned. Should it have happened that Paul stumbled and fell he could have hit his head on the hard road surface or on a rock and suffered a concussion with mild traumatic brain injury. Such a fall could have caused him to "see stars"[190], which may explain the bright light he saw.

It is also possible that he was struck by lightning – the bright light that he saw – which must have caused him to become concussed.[191]

A concussion is usually called a closed brain injury since the skull was not penetrated. The traumatic brain injury (TBI) occurs when the brain is jolted within the skull due to a fall or a knock against the head. The bump against the head, whether from a heavy

---

expression σεληνιάζομαι (*seleniazomai*) – to suffer from "moon sickness" – is used for epilepsy.
[190] Zillmer, *Principles of Neuropsychol0gy*, 379; Spoor, "Concussion and your Vision".
[191] Lezak, *Neuropsychological Assessment*, 226–27.

7. PAUL'S VIVIONS AND REVELATIONS

object or the ground during a fall, causes the brain to move rapidly within the skull and bounce back.[192]

A mild TBI may not impair the victim's cognitive functioning in the long run, but a number of other conditions may result. These conditions may be due to the tearing of nerve fibers, bleeding in the brain (called hematomas), oedema (swelling in the brain), brain tumors that develop and meningiomas (benign tumors within the meninges, the soft protective layer between the brain and the skull).[193]

Some of the consequences of a mild TBI include the following:

- Epilepsy, especially left temporal lobe epilepsy, mostly due to scar tissue or tumors within the brain;[194]
- Headaches, including migraines;[195]
- Amnesia;[196]
- Temporary blindness;[197]
- Persistent problems with vision;[198]

---

[192] Zillmer, *Principles of Neuropsychology*, 371, 375.

[193] Zillmer, *Principles of Neuropsychology*, 359; Kolb and Wishaw, *Fundamentals of Human Neuropsychology*, 759; Coetzer, "Auditory Hallucinations", 15.

[194] Zillmer, *Principles of Neuropsychology*, 379; Kolb and Wishaw, *Fundamentals of Human Neuropsychology* 757; Webb, "Auditory Hallucinations", 539; White, "Concussion"; Hishaw, "Concussion"; McAllister & Ferrell, 2002: 357; Lamar *et al.* 2014: 110–11.

[195] Webb, "Auditory Hallucinations", 539.

[196] Hishaw, "Concussion"; Fisher, "Seizures".

[197] Granacher, 2008: 285-287; Kaye & Herskowitz, 1986: 206; Spoor, "Concussion" Metcalf and Bass, "Head Injuries".

[198] Kaye and Herskowitz, "Transient post-traumatic cortical blindness" 206; Hishaw, "Concussion"; Spoor, "Concussion".

7. PAUL'S VIVIONS AND REVELATIONS

- Personality changes, including mania, depression, increased aggression and paranoia;[199]
- The development of Parkinson's Disease with its characteristic muscle tremors and rigidity;[200]
- Auditory and visionary hallucinations;[201] and
- Some patients develop "excessive verbal output, ... hypergraphia, altered sexuality (usually hyposexuality), and intensified mental life (obsessional cognitive and spiritual/religious ideation)."[202]

This condition is also known as the Geschwind Syndrome.[203]

It may be clear from the foregoing that Paul's "thorn in the flesh" may well have been caused by a mild traumatic brain injury, contracted when he had a serious fall on the Damascus Road. This TBI may be an explanation for his temporary blindness, his shocked condition after the event (perhaps due to amnesia), his possible eye problems, his possible hallucinations during which he "saw" and "heard" the risen Christ, his possible epilepsy, his possible OBE and his personality profile. He needed a rest period of three years in Arabia and Damascus after his experience on the road to Damascus before he recuperated enough to start a career as travelling missionary (Gal 1: 17–18).

---

[199] Kolb and Wishaw, 2009: 756; Lezak, 2012: 247; Nicholl, "Neuropsychiatric Sequelae", 247.

[200] Zillmer, *Principles of Neuropsychology*, 424; Crane et al., "Association of Traumatic Brain Injury'.

[201] Granacher, 2008: 172-173; Nicholl, 2009: 247; Webb, "Auditory Hallucinations", 539; Greenwald, "Hallucinations and Delusions"; McAllister and Ferrell, "Evaluation and Treatment of Psychosis", 357.

[202] Lezak, *Neuropsychological Assessment*, 246.

[203] BENSON, "The Geschwind Syndrome", 411–21; Devinsky and Schachter: "Norman Geschwind's Contribution".

7. PAUL'S VIVIONS AND REVELATIONS

Paul's personality traits are congruous with a TBI, as well as with the Geschwind syndrome. The symptoms of this syndrome are as follows:

- Hyperreligiosity – an extreme interest in religion and philosophy;
- Hypergraphia – a tendency for compulsive writing;
- Atypical sexuality – usually a lack of interest in sexual activities;
- Circumstantiality – the tendency to repeat ideas; and
- Intensified mental life – much introspection and extreme emotional reactions[204]

Paul's interest and even obsession with religious matters cannot be denied. When reading his letters in one go one gets the impression of an author who could almost not stop his outpouring of ideas. He was very verbose and almost fanatical about the message he wanted to convey. He reacted aggressively and suspiciously against those who did not agree with his ideas and called the curse of God upon them (Gal 1: 8–9; 2: 13). Although he was not against marriage, he was not married himself and seemingly had no interest in sex.[205] These traits are consistent with the symptoms of a mild TBI and the Geschwind Syndrome.

New Religion

When one compares the views of Paul and the gospel writers with those of the Jewish followers of Jesus, one must conclude that Paul actually invented a totally new religion, which was more in tune

---

[204] Benson: " The Geschwind Syndrome" 411–21" ; Devinsky and Schachter, "Norman Geschwind's Contribution".
[205] Sanders, "Paul, the Apostle, Saint".

7. PAUL'S VIVIONS AND REVELATIONS

with the gentile and pagan world of his day than with Judaism.[206] This new religion, in time, became Christianity. This religion's view of Jesus Christ was, in due course, precisely formulated in a number of creeds, some of which were quoted at the beginning of this book.

Paul's views regarding a deified Christ would have not have been so strange to his Gentile converts since the classical world was familiar with mythical figures who were demi-gods, in many cases the offspring of Zeus, the chief deity of the Greeks, who impregnated quite a number of earthly maidens. These sons, including the strong man Hercules, became mythological demi-gods.[207] The Egyptian pharaohs and the Roman emperors also regarded themselves as sons or descendants of some or other deity.

In this process, Paul transformed the Old Testament concept of "son of God" as applied to the kings of the house of David (Ps 2: 7, *etcetera*), into a Greek concept. In other words, he ignored the use in the Old Testament of this title and declared Jesus to be the *only* Son of God (Rom 2: 2–4) – which later led to the Christian dogma of the divine trinity consisting of Father, Son and Holy Spirit.

Paul also gave the title "Christ" a new meaning. This word means "anointed" and as such it was applied in the Old Testament to kings, prophets and priests who were the anointed of God (Lev 4: 3; Num 3: 3; 1 Sam 2: 10, 35; 1 Sam 12: 3; 1 Sam 16: 13; 1 Sam 24: 7; 1 Kgs 1: 39 *etcetera*).[208] The Hebrew word for "anointed" is מָשִׁיחַ (*mashiyach*). The English word "messiah" is a transliteration. Paul uses the Greek translation of this title (Χριστός – *Christos*) in his letters as if it were a proper name. When referring to Jesus, he often simply calls him Christ. For him, therefore, Jesus was the only anointed of God.

---

[206] Wilson, *How Jesus Became Christian*, 113–16.
[207] Grayling, *The God Argument*, 31.
[208] Fredriksen, *Jesus of Nazareth*, 119.

7. PAUL'S VIVIONS AND REVELATIONS

That Jesus was born from a virgin is a Christian article of faith. Paul never mentioned it in his epistles and he merely wrote that Jesus was "born to a woman" (Gal 4: 4) and that he was "born of the seed of David" (Rom 1: 3). Had he been aware of the purported miraculous birth of Jesus, he surely would have mentioned it. After all, he frequently mentioned Jesus' crucifixion and resurrection. Had he known of Jesus' so-called virgin birth, it would have bolstered his contention that Jesus was a divine being.

The Gospels of Matthew and Luke, in an endeavor to support Paul's idea that Jesus was God incarnate, invented a miraculous birth from a virgin. They were certainly aware of examples in the ancient world of heroes and demi-gods whose mothers were virgins who were somehow impregnated by a god and they placed Jesus alongside these mythological and legendary heroes. It has already been pointed out that the nativity stories of Matthew and Luke are pious inventions. Jesus' virgin birth, although it is regarded as an article of faith, is destined to be relegated to the realm of myths.

Paul's promise of a blissful afterlife with God and Christ would also have been attractive to people in the ancient world since the classical Greek religion contained no such promise; the deceased were merely thought of as "witless ghosts" in the underworld.[209]

It is possible and probable that Paul was influenced by the Egyptian religion in which much was made of the afterlife and the judgment of the deceased. In the Roman Empire there were many adherents of the Egyptian religion and many more people would have been familiar with its teachings. For the Egyptians, only royalty and the elite had any chance of reaching a heavenly afterlife when their corpses were mummified before burial.[210] Paul's teachings would have been attractive to poor and common folk with

---

[209] Pollard and Adkins, "Greek Religion".
[210] Baines, "Egyptian Religion".

7. PAUL'S VIVIONS AND REVELATIONS

his promise that resurrection and life everlasting was due to all believers, irrespective of nationality, social class or gender (Gal 3: 28–29).

Whereas Jesus expected the Kingdom of God to arrive during his lifetime, Paul had to adjust this expectation because it did not happen that way. Paul, therefore, transferred the coming of the Kingdom into the near future when the risen Jesus Christ was supposed to return unexpectedly, like "a thief in the night" (1 Thess 5: 1–4).[211]

Paul's new religion made use of rituals – just as the pagan religions of his day – in order to reenact the "mysteries" of which he had visions and revelations. The mystery religions of those times initiated new converts with all sorts of, often terrifying, rituals and ordeals in which certain aspects of the tales regarding the gods of these religions were ritually repeated. In Paul's proto-Christianity, he introduced the ritual of the Eucharist or Lord's supper in which the death and resurrection of Jesus Christ were reenacted in order to give his converts an experience in which they could become one with their savior (1 Cor 11: 23–34). It has to be pointed out that his version of the way in which Jesus was supposed to have instituted this symbolic commemorative meal differs in many details of the representation of this event in the gospels where Jesus enjoyed the Passover with his disciples before being arrested (Mark 14: 22–26; Mat 26: 26–30; Luke 22:15–20).[212] The Didache's description of the Lord's Supper (Did 9 and 10) also diverges widely from Paul's invention of the Eucharist.

It has to be emphasized that Paul must have been very sincere regarding his convictions. He did not deliberately start a new religion; he was convinced that his visions and revelations were

---

[211] Fredriksen, *Jesus of Nazareth*, 81.
[212] Wolmarans, "Jesus, die Heroïese Patroon, en ons." 196–224.

7. PAUL'S VIVIONS AND REVELATIONS

genuine and that Christ really appeared to him and called him to become his apostle or representative. His mixed Jewish and Greek background led him to propagate ideas that were a combination of ideas from the Old Testament and paganism. His numerous allusions to the Old Testament gave his message a link to an ancient and respected tradition, but he also introduced ideas that were familiar and acceptable to his gentile converts, including the introduction of Christ as a divine figure who was resurrected from the grave and was taken up into the heavens. This all amounts to nothing but a pious but unfounded myth, dished out upon a receptive world.

The Jewish followers of Jesus, on the other hand, did not regard their religion as anything but Judaism and they constituted just another religious group within Judaism. Jesus, their teacher, only explained the Torah and he definitely did not intend to start a new religion.[213]

The converts to Paul's new religion, who converted Jesus Christ into a divine figure, and the Jewish followers of Jesus formed, therefore, two distinct and separate groups. The book of Acts tried to link the two movements as two varieties of the same religious movement, which started on Pentecost, but that is an oversimplification. Even in Acts, one can read of differences of opinion between these two rival groups (cf Acts 15 and 22). In his letter to the Galatians, Paul argued that his converts ought not to follow the Jewish Torah. According to him, Christ liberated those who believe in him from the fetters of the Law. The leadership and members of the original Jerusalem congregation, on the other hand, could not accept this point of view and they continued to follow the prescriptions of the Old Testament, as explained by Jesus when he was alive, while continuing to worship in the Jerusalem temple.[214]

---

[213] Wilson, *How Jesus Became Christian*, 74.
[214] Wilson, *How Jesus Became Christian*, 74–84.

7. PAUL'S VIVIONS AND REVELATIONS

It seems that this division between Paul's followers and the Jewish followers of Jesus became visible even in Corinth. In his first letter to the Corinthians, Paul mentions that he was informed of divisions in that church: "That is, that some of you say, I am of Paul; some say, I am of Apollos; some say, I am of Cephas; and some say, I am Christ's" (1 Cor 1: 12). Those who belonged to the party of Cephas (Peter) and of Christ were most probably the Jewish followers of Jesus, while the party of Paul consisted of his pagan converts. The people who supported Apollos were most probably inspired by the teachings of John the Baptist.

Paul also condemned and cursed those who did not agree with his version of the gospel in the strongest terms –and he especially had the Jewish followers of Jesus in mind:

> "But even though we, or an angel from heaven, should preach to you any gospel other than that which we preached to you, let him be cursed. As we have said before, so I now say again: if any man preaches to you any gospel other than that which you received, let him be cursed" (Gal 1: 8–9).

That Paul regarded his movement indeed as separate from that of the Jewish followers of Jesus is clear from various passages where he warned against "false apostles" and those who required of converts from paganism to be circumcised and, in effect, adopt a Jewish lifestyle (2 Cor 11: 5; 2 Cor 11: 13–15; 2 Cor 13:11; Gal 5:2–4). In Tit 1: 10–14 and 3: 9 he (or his secretary who wrote the letter on his behalf) warned against those Jewish converts who propagated "Jewish fables and commandments of men" and held themselves busy with "foolish questionings, genealogies, strife, and disputes about the law [of Moses]".

Gager came to the same conclusion after examining Paul's letters and his attitude towards the Jews. According to him, the

7. PAUL'S VIVIONS AND REVELATIONS

traditional reading of Paul was that he had profound differences with the Jews as such. His real opponents were actually the other apostles within the Jewish Jesus Movement.[215] From 2 Cor 11: 10–22 it is clear that these "false apostles" were Jewish – in other words, the original followers or pupils of Jesus.

Paul reported that he had convinced the apostles in Jerusalem of his insights and that they agreed that the apostles would concentrate their efforts on the Jews, while Paul and Barnabas would bring the gospel to the gentile world (Gal 2: 1–10). That does not quite seem to be the case. This meeting is also reported in Acts 15 and if the resolution of the meeting is reported correctly (Acts 15: 28–29), it seems that the apostles agreed to keep the *status quo* intact, namely that Jewish followers of Jesus continue to follow the laws of the Old Testament, while Paul's gentile converts were only required to adhere to the requirements set for gentile proselytes, as before. These proselytes were welcome to participate in the worship of the God of Israel, but they were not compelled to adhere to all the Old Testament laws.[216] In other words: Paul did not really convince the apostles of his ideas and they actually agreed to disagree.

Paul's new religion was the product of the mind of an intellectual giant. Paul was, no doubt, a very gifted writer and orator who managed to forge a credible new intellectual construct out of elements of the Jewish religion, the teachings and life of Jesus of Nazareth, pagan religions, Greek philosophy, together with his visions, revelations and hallucinations regarding Jesus. That this intellectual system became, in time, Christianity and the biggest religion in the history of the world is no mean feat.

---

[215] Gager, "Paul's Contradictions".
[216] Fredriksen, *Jesus of Nazareth,* 263; Botha, "Proseliet & Proselitisme", 904–05.

CHAPTER 8

EVALUATION

The Character and Personality of Jesus
When one reads the gospels carefully one gets a less than flattering picture of the character of Jesus – which does not fit the conventional view that he was a perfect human being, without any sin or flaw (Heb 5: 9; Heb 7: 26–28; Heb 9: 28; 1 Pet 2: 22). That is, to say, if the following reports of the words and actions of Jesus are accurate and factual.

When Jesus attended a wedding feast at the town of Cana, he was rather rude towards his mother (John 2: 4).

According to Matt 8: 21–22, somebody wanted to follow Jesus, but requested some time to bury his father first. Jesus gave a very inconsiderate reply: "Follow me, and leave the dead to bury their own dead."

A friendly Pharisee invited Jesus to a meal. When Jesus failed to wash his hands before the meal, his host asked why he hadn't done so. Jesus thereupon insulted his host and levelled a number of curses upon the Pharisees in general (Luke 11: 37–44). This does not tie in well with his message of neighborly love and forgiveness.

To Thomas Jesus said: "I am the way, the truth, and the life. No one comes to the Father, but by me" (John 14: 6). If Jesus really uttered these words, then it must be a sign that he had an over-inflated sense of his own importance. Christians often quote these words to "prove" that Christianity is the only true religion. But if it really is so that no one can know or reach

8. EVALUATION

God without believing in Jesus then one must also wonder how it was possible for the prophets of the Old Testament, who lived centuries before Jesus, to know God and to speak for God, as they claimed.

The same narcissistic attitude is evident in these words of Jesus to his disciples: "He who hates me, hates my Father also" (John 15: 23). He is also reported as saying: "He that is not with me is against me" (Luke 11: 23).

Jesus taught pacifism on the one hand. In the Sermon on the Mount, he said: "But I tell you, don't resist him who is evil; but whoever strikes you on your right cheek, turn to him the other also" (Matt 5: 39). On the other hand, he was not averse to use violence himself:

> "He found in the temple those who sold oxen, sheep, and doves, and the changers of money sitting. He made a whip of cords, and threw all out of the temple, both the sheep and the oxen; and he poured out the changers' money, and overthrew their tables" (John 2: 14–15).

Jesus gave this testimonial about himself (if reported correctly): "Take my yoke on you, and learn from me, for I am humble and lowly in heart; and you will find rest for your souls" (Matt 11: 29). No person who is really humble will boast about it in this manner.

Jesus could be rude towards non-Jews. When a Canaanite woman from Phoenicia beseeched him to heal her daughter, he initially ignored her. When his disciples begged him to listen to her, he answered that he was only interested in helping Israelites and he even compared the Gentiles with "dogs" (Matt 15: 21–28).

8. EVALUATION

In Mark 11: 12–20 we are told of Jesus who was hungry and spotted a fig tree. He expected to find fruit on the tree, although it was not the season for figs. He thereupon cursed the tree and it withered and died. It is totally unclear what the meaning of this pointless miracle was, since Jesus did nothing to benefit any other human being. On the other hand, he probably caused some damage to the owner of the land on which the tree was growing and who depended upon the tree for a crop of figs. This incident – if it really happened – shows a less desirable character trait of Jesus, namely anger against a fig tree for no rational reason. It is, however, also possible that this tree was anyway diseased and dried up on its own and that some of Jesus' followers connected that to Jesus' presence on the scene.

When his disciples complained about the fact that his head and feet were anointed with an expensive ointment by a woman and that the money could have been better used for charity, Jesus retorted: "For you always have the poor with you, and whenever you want to, you can do them good; but you will not always have me" (Mark 14: 7). This sounds rather self-centered and arrogant.

The people who knew him best, the inhabitants of Nazareth where he grew up, did not think much of him and they even tried to push him over a cliff, accusing him of being a fraud (Matt 13: 57; Luke 4: 28–30). There were those who regarded him as "a glutton and a drunkard, a friend of tax collectors and sinners" (Matt 11: 19).

Was Jesus really the God-like figure and perfect, sinless human being as portrayed elsewhere in the gospels and the rest of the New Testament? The incidents mentioned here don't seem to agree with these ideas and it seems as if Jesus rather had a narcissistic, haughty and arrogant streak. These characteristics and behaviors can only be attributed to the fact that Jesus saw

8. EVALUATION

himself as a very special person – the king-in-waiting of Israel and God's favorite son.

In addition, there are sayings of Jesus from which it is clear that he never thought of himself as a divine personage. To a rich young man, he said: ""Why do you call me good? No one is good but one, that is, God" (Matt 19: 17). He also said: "The Father is greater than I" (John 14: 28). When a teacher of the law asked Jesus which of the laws was the most important, Jesus quoted from the Old Testament:

> "The greatest is, 'Hear, Israel, the Lord our God, the Lord is one: you shall love the Lord your God with all your heart, and with all your soul, and with all your mind, and with all your strength.' This is the primary commandment." (Mark 12: 29–30).

If Jesus stressed that "the Lord is one", then there is no place for a divine Trinity.

This is also what Paul teaches. In 1 Cor 15: 24–28, Paul gave an explanation of what will happen after Judgment Day "when He [Christ] will deliver up the kingdom to God, the Father," with the result that "the Son will also himself be subjected to him who subjected all things to him, that God may be all in all" – which means the Christ will abdicate his position as Son of God and that amounts to an abolishment of the divine Trinity.

The fact that Jesus submitted to baptism by John the Baptist demonstrates that he did not see himself as a sinless human being. John was a prophet who emulated the Old Testament figure of Elijah and Jesus – according to Matthew – even claimed that John was a resurrected or reincarnated Elijah (Matt 1: 13–14; Matt 11: 14; Matt 17: 10–13). John called people

8. EVALUATION

to repentance and baptized them in the river Jordan as a symbolic act to cleanse them of their sins (Matt 3: 1–6; Luke 3: 3). In this, he followed other Jewish groups, such as the Essenes, who also practiced baptism or used ritual baths.[217]

Jesus' baptism by John (Matt 3: 13–16; Mark 1: 9; Luke 3: 21) is usually explained as a demonstration of his solidarity with repentant sinners, although he himself had no sins and had no real need to be baptized. That is a rather convoluted explanation and it finds no justification in the biblical texts. The most straightforward and rational explanation is that Jesus saw himself as a sinner and that he needed to confess his sins and his subservience to God in public by being baptized. With this action he also demonstrated his acceptance of John's message and his identification with the party made up of John's supporters, mostly Essenes or Nazoreans.

Which Type of Christ?

Which of these two religious movements are to be believed regarding Jesus? Do we believe Paul, who did not know Jesus personally, who had all sorts of visions and revelations – most probably hallucinations that could not be corroborated by anyone – and who made a mythological figure out of Jesus of Nazareth? Do we believe the gospel stories, including the virgin birth and Jesus' resurrection from the dead and ascension into heaven? Or do we believe the early Jewish "Christians" or Ebionites and Nazoreans of Jerusalem and Judea who knew Jesus and his apostles personally and regarded him as a mere mortal man?

---

[217] Encyclopaedia Britannica, "John the Baptist, Saint".

8. EVALUATION

I am convinced that nobody can deny that these Jewish followers of Jesus deserve to be regarded as being much more credible and reliable than Paul and the authors of the gospels.

One cannot but wonder what the reaction of Jesus of Nazareth would have been if he had known during his lifetime that he would later be regarded as the eternal Son of God, the second Person of the Triune God, the savior of the world and the Cosmic Judge. What would he have said had he known that his birthday would be celebrated by Christians and non-Christians alike each year around the date of the winter solstice, the old pagan feast of the rebirth of the sun?

There are, indeed, expressions placed in Jesus' mouth by the gospel writers to the effect that he regarded himself as the equal of his heavenly Father but they can safely be seen as theological pronouncements and propaganda from the perspective of a number of decades after his death – and not as authentic utterances made by him.

We can imagine that he would have been horrified if he knew how he would be deified after his death and placed on the same level as the many sons of Zeus or on the same level as the Egyptian Pharaohs and Roman emperors who expected people to worship them as gods. As a Jew, he definitely would have regarded this deification as utter blasphemy and idolatry, while he merely regarded himself as the king-in-waiting of the restored nation of Israel and God's representative in a future theocratic dispensation.

It must be remembered, though, that the gospel writers never had the intention of writing objective biographies of Jesus; their writings were intended as propaganda and theological interpretations for the young Christian movement, started by Paul. They purposely invented nativity stories and resurrection stories along the lines of pagan myths to portray Jesus as a divine

8. EVALUATION

figure and to make him acceptable to the people in the Roman Empire.[218]

The conclusion must be made that the essential feature of the conventional or orthodox Christian faith, which regards Jesus Christ as the eternal Son of God, as the son of a virgin, as the second Person of the divine Trinity, as the savior of the world and as the judge on Judgment Day, rests upon a fallacy or a fantasy introduced by Paul with his visions and revelations and which was repeated by the gospel writers. Jesus was, in reality, nothing but a mortal man and his death on the cross, although tragic and cruel, had absolutely no religious or theological implications. He certainly did not die to save those who believe in him from eternal punishment in hell. He was also not miraculously resurrected from his tomb to pave the way for believers towards heavenly bliss.[219]

Although we cannot agree with Paul's message regarding Jesus, the ideas of the Ebionites are also not acceptable in all respects. If it is so that they expected Jesus to return soon as a reincarnated personage – just as John the Baptist was declared by Jesus to be a reincarnated Elijah – then we must conclude that they were misguided in this respect.

In 2010, the Canadian physician George Burden posed the question: "Did epilepsy lead to the foundation of Christianity?" His answered his own question in the affirmative and concluded that Christianity would not have become the official religion of the Roman Empire if Paul "had not suffered from a seizure disorder."[220] It definitely seems as if he made a valid point.

---

[218] Wolmarans, "Jesus, die Heroïese Patroon, en Ons", 196–224.
[219] Wilson, *How Jesus Became Christian*, 241–48.
[220] Burden, "Did epilepsy lead to the foundation of Christianity?"

8. EVALUATION

It may be added that a seemingly insignificant incident, namely a Jew having a fall while travelling on a road and bumping his head, seems to have produced profound and decisive global consequences and steered the history of the world in a totally new direction because this Jew's head injury caused him to have hallucinations and to start a new world religion, namely Christianity. One can only wonder: how would history have developed if he never had that fall? How would humanity have developed if Christianity never appeared on the scene and became the dominant religion in the late Roman Empire?[1]

Jesus' Personality and Impact
When evaluating the personality, ideas and impact of Jesus of Nazareth, one has to conclude that he must have been a very dynamic and charismatic leader – otherwise he would not have been able to build up a large following and movement that continued after his death and otherwise people would not have thought it worthwhile to collect memories about his ministry and compile a number of biographies, decades after his death.

Although Jesus was a charismatic figure that made a lasting impression on his contemporaries, he certainly had some delusions of grandeur. He regarded himself as God's chosen instrument to drive the Romans away and re-establish the Davidic dynasty in Jerusalem. When the realities of the times are taken into consideration it must be clear that he did not have the slightest chance of realizing his dream. The military might of Rome was simply too great – as was amply demonstrated a few decades after his death during the Jewish War of AD 66–70 when Jerusalem was destroyed and the Jews were utterly humiliated.

8. EVALUATION

One may indeed wonder: how much could the lingering influence of Jesus and his message about the kingdom of God may have prompted the Jews to start a war against the Roman occupiers of their country in AD 66, forty years after his crucifixion? It is, now, many centuries after the event, certainly impossible to give a definite answer to this question. It is, however, quite possible that his message about the kingdom of God could have had an influence on the Jewish leaders who started a revolt.

If Paul did not appear on the scene and turned Jesus into a divine figure on account of his visions or hallucinations, Jesus would have remained a footnote in the history books. Paul's efforts as a missionary and an administrator caused an alternative Jesus Movement, the Christian Church, to be organized, which would, in time, become the most successful religious group in the history of mankind. This religious group is, though, doomed to become extinct in due course because it will become clearer and clearer, as time goes on, that it is built upon a series of fallacies and improbable myths and amounts to a pious deception.

Jesus of Nazareth will be remembered as a wise teacher and a benefactor of his fellow men who made a lasting impact upon his followers, but also as a tragic revolutionary, a deluded messiah. He, nevertheless, deserves to be commemorated as an exceptional figure in Jewish history.

BIBLIOGRAPHY

Editions of the Bible
Passages from the Bible are quoted from the *World English Bible* as found on a CD with the title *The Bible Collection, Deluxe Edition*, and published by ValuSoft, a division of THQ Inc, Waconia MN, 2002.

The above-mentioned CD also contains the Hebrew text of the Old Testament and the Greek text of the New Testament, as well as *Strong's Complete Greek & Hebrew Lexicon*. Other lexica utilized are mentioned under the heading of Other Publications.

In addition, the following editions of the biblical text in the original languages were consulted:

Elliger, K. and W. Rudolph, eds. *Biblia Hebraica Stuttgartensia*. Stuttgart: Deutsche Bibelgesellschaft, 1997.
Nestle, E. and E. Nestle, eds. *Novum Testamentum Graece*. Stuttgart: Deutsche Bibelstiftung, 1981.

The text of the ancient Greek translation of the Old Testament, the so-called *Septuagint (LXX)*, was downloaded from the following website:
https://www.academic-bible.com/en/online-bibles/septuagint-lxx/read-the-bible-text/

The text of the ancient Latin translation of the New Testament, the Vulgate, was found in the following publication:

Wordsworth, Iohannes et A.M. White, eds., *Novum Testamentum Latine: Secundum Editionem Sancti Hieronymi, ad Codicum Mauscrip-torum Fidem Recensuerunt*. London: Oxford University Press, 1955.

Other Publications

Allen, Richard Hinckley. *Star Names: Their Lore and Meaning.* New York: Dover, 1963.

American Psychiatric Association. *Diagnostic and Statistical Manual of Mental Disorders, Fifth Edition: DSM-5.* Washington: American Psychiatric Publishing, 2013.

Aminoff, M.J., ed. *Encyclopedia of the Neurological Sciences.* New York: Elsevier Science, 2003.

Anon, "First the Munchies then the Mania". *Medical Brief,* 18.02.2015. http://www.medicalbrief.co.za/archives/first-the-munchies-then-the-mania/

Akin, J. "7 Clues Tell Us Precisely When Jesus Died (The Year, Month, Day, and Hour Revealed)". http://www.ncregister.com/blog/jimmy-akin./when-precisely-did-jesus-die-the-year-month-day-and-hour-revealed

Aristotle: *On the Heavens, Book 1.* Translated by W.K.C. Guthrie, Loeb Classical Library, Harvard University Press, 1939. https://hedberg.ccnysites.cuny.edu/PHYS454/aristotle-on-the-heavens.pdf

Armstrong, Karen. *Fields of Blood: Religion and the History of Violence.* London: Vintage, 2014.

Arndt, W.F. and F.W. Gingrich, A *Greek-English Lexicon of the New Testament and Other Early Christian Literature.* Chicago: University of Chicago Press, 1957.

Baigent, Michael et al. *The Holy Blood and the Holy Grail.* London: Corgi, 1993.

Baines, J.R. "Egyptian Religion". In *Encyclopædia Britannica,* 2010.

Belgic Confession, The. http://gksa.org.za/pdf/eng%20documents/belgic%20confession.pdf

Benson, D.F. "The Geschwind Syndrome". *Advances in Neurology.* 1991; 55: 41,1–21.

BIBLIOGRAPHY

Botha, A.N. "Proseliet & Proselitisme". In *Christelike Kernensiklopedie*, edited by Frits Gaum et al. Wellington: Lux Verbi, 2008.
Bowman, Robert Jr. *Historical Jesus Outlines and Notes* - Credo House 2009.
https://mail.google.com/mail/u/0/?tab=rm&ogbl#trash/FMfc gzGmvnzSHbtWgWzmSvvdPsMFwVKp
Burden, G. "Did Epilepsy Lead to the Foundation of Christianity? *Life as a Human*, 30 June, 2010.
http://lifeasahuman.com/2010/mind-spirit/spirituality-and-religion/did-epilepsy-lead-to-the-foundation-of-christianity/
Burstein, Dan, ed. *Secrets of the Code: The Unauthorized Guide to the Mysteries Beyond The Da Vinci Code*. London: Weidenfeld and Nicholson, 2004.
Clark, P. et al. eds. *Lippincott's Illustrated Reviews: Pharmacology*. Baltimore: Wolters Kluwer Health, 2012.
Coetzer, R. "Auditory Hallucinations Secondary to a Right Frontal Meningioma". *Journal of Neuropsychiatry and Clinical Neuroscience*, 26.3, Summer 2014.
http://www.pubfacts.com/detail/25093770/auditory-hallucinations-secondary-to-a-right-frontal-meningioma.
Cohn, H. *The Trial and Death of Jesus*. Old Saybrook, Ct: Konecky & Konecky, 1980.
Craighead, W.E. and C.B. Nemeroff, eds. *The Corsini Encyclopedia of Psychology and Behavioral Science, Volume 4*. Hoboken, NJ: John Wiley & Sons, 2002.
Crane, P. et al. "Association of Traumatic Brain Injury with Late-Life Neurodegenerative Conditions and Neuropathologic Findings". *JAMA Neurology* 2016; Doi: 10.1001/Jamaneurol.2016.1948.
http://www.medpagetoday.com/neurology/headtrauma/59034?xid=nl_mpt_dhe_2016-07-13&eun=g581939d0r
Delsemme, A.H. "Comet". In *Encyclopædia Britannica*, 2010.
Devinsky, J. and S. Schachter. "Norman Geschwind's Contribution to the Understanding of Behavioral Changes in Temporal Lobe

BIBLIOGRAPHY

Epilepsy: The February 1974 Lecture". *Epilepsy & Behavior.* **15** (4): 417–24.
https://pubmed.ncbi.nlm.nih.gov/19640791/

Dann, Moshe, "The Essenes and the Origins of Christianity: How the Essenes played a part in history". Jerusalem Post: 13 July, 2018.
https://www.jpost.com/jerusalem-report/the-essenes-and-the-origins-of-christianity-562442

Duling, Dennis, "The Jewish World of Jesus". In *The New Testament: An Introduction.* San Diego, Harcourt Brace Jovanovich, 1982, pp. 4–35.
https://pages.charlotte.edu/james-tabor/the-jewish-world-of-jesus-an-overview/

Eisenman, R. *James the Brother of Jesus: The Key to Unlocking the Secrets of Early Christianity and the Dead Sea Scrolls.* Harmondsworth: Penguin, 1997.

Elliot, B. et al. "Delusions, Illusions and Hallucinations in Epilepsy: Elementary Phenomena." *Epilepsy Res,* Aug 2009: 162–171.
http://www.ncbi.nlm.nih.gov/pubmed/19423297

Elkins, N.T. "Roman Emperor Nerva's Reform of the Jewish Tax: How Jews and Christians Became Further Differentiated under Nerva". *Biblical Archaeology*, 22.05.2017.
http://www.biblicalarchaeology.org/daily/ancient-cultures/daily-life-and-practice/roman-emperor-nervas-reform-of-the-jewish-tax/

Encylopaedia Britannica, 2010: "Census".
——. "Dehydration".
——. "Didache".
——. "Drug Cult".
——. "Ebionites".
——. "Essenes".
——. "James, The Letter of".
——. "Jewish Revolt, First".
——. "John The Baptist, Saint".
——. "Judas Iscariot".

BIBLIOGRAPHY

-----. "Maccabees.".
-----. "Marijuana".
-----. "Nazarenes".
-----. "Opium".
-----. "Pontius Pilate".
-----. "Simon The Apostle, Saint."
Encyclopedia.Com. "Historical Jesus".
    https://www.encyclopedia.com/religion/encyclopedias-almanacs-transcripts-and-maps/historical-jesus
Eusebius of Caesarea. *Historia Ecclesiastica, Liberi I & II*.
    http://www.documentacatholicaomnia.eu/03d/0265-0339,_eusebius_caesariensis,_church_history,_en.pdf
----- Ευσεβιου Καισαρειας, Εκκλησιαστικη Ιστορια.
    http://www.documentacatholicaomnia.eu/03d/0265-0339,_Eusebius_Caesariensis,_Historia_Ecclesiastica,_GR.pdf
Fiore, K. 2016. Cannabidiol may Cut Seizure Severity in Refractory Epilepsy. *Medpage Today,* 6 December 2016.
    http://www.medpagetoday.com/meetingcoverage/aes/61888
Fisher, R.S. "Seizures From Head Trauma". *Stanford Epilepsy Center.* 2015
    http://neurology.stanford.edu/epilepsy/patientcare/videos/e
Fredriksen, Paula. *Jesus of Nazareth, King of the Jews: A Jewish Life and the Emergence of Christianity.* London: Macmillan. 2000.
Freke, T. and P. Gandy. *Jesus and the Goddess: The Secret Teachings of the Original Christians.* London: Thorsons, 2002.
-----. The Jesus Mysteries: Was the Original Jesus a Pagan God? London: Thorsons, 1999.
Gager, J.G. "Paul's Contradictions: Can they be Resolved?" In *Paul: Jewish Law And Early Christianity*, edited by M Warker, Biblical Archeological Society, 2012, 1–15.
Gaum, F. et al., eds. *Christelike Kernensiklopedie.* Wellington: Lux Verbi, 2008.

BIBLIOGRAPHY

Gertoux, Gérard. *Herod the Great and Jesus : Chronological, Historical and Archaelogical Evidence.* 2015. file:///C:/Users/User/Downloads/Herod_the_Great_and _Jesus _Chronological.pdf

Goulder, M. *St. Paul Versus St. Peter: A Tale of two Missions.* Atlanta: John Knox, 1995.

Granacher, R.P. *Traumatic Brain Injury: Methods for Clinical and Forensic Neuropsychiatric Assessment.* Boca Raton Fl: CRC, 2008.

Gray, G.B., transl. "The Psalms of Solomon, Translated from Greek and Syriac Manuscripts". In *The Apocrypha and Pseudepigrapha of the Old Testament in English*, edited by R.H. Charles. Oxford: Clarendon, 1913. http://wesley.nnu.edu/sermons-essays-books/noncanonical-literature/noncanonical-literature-ot-pseudepigrapha/the-psalms-of-solomon/

Grayling, A.C. *The God Argument: The Case Against Religion and for Humanism.* London: Bloomsbury, 2014.

Greenwald, B.D. "Hallucinations and Delusions after a Brain Injury". *Brainline.Org.,* 2015. http://brainline.org.content/2010/12/hallucinations-and-delusions-after-a-brain-injury.html

Greenwood, S. and R. Airey. *The Complete Illustrated encyclopedia of Witchcraft & Magic.* London: Hermes House, 2007.

Hancock, Graham. *Supernatural: Meetings with the Ancient Teachers of Mankind.* London: Century 2005.

Harris, Sam. *The End of Faith: Religion, Terror and the Future of Reason.* London: The Free Press, 2005.

Heidelberg Catechism, The http://gksa.org.za/pdf/eng%20documents/heidelberg%20catechism.pdf

Hendricks, Obrey M., Jr. "The Gospel According to John". In In Coogan, Michael D. et al. Eds. The New Oxford

Annotated Bible (3rd ed.). Peabody, Massachusetts: Hendrickson, 2007.

Hishaw, G.A. "Concussion and Epilepsy: What is the Link?" *Practical Neurology.* May/June 2012.
http://practicalneurology.com/2012/06/concussion-and-epilepsy-what-is-the-link

Hitchens, C. *God is not Great: The Case Against Religion.* London: Atlantic, 2007.

Hoffman, R.E. et al. "Transcranial Magnetic Stimulation of Left Temporal Cortex and Medication-Resistant Auditory Hallucinations". *Arch Gen Psychiatry,* Vol 60, January 2003: 49–56.
http://www.neuro.hk/img/tmshallucinationsschizophrenia.pdf

Holford, Patrick. *How To Quit Without Feeling S**T.* London: Piatkus, 2008.

Humphreys, C.J. and W.G. Waddington, "The Jewish Calendar, a Lunar Eclipse and the Date of Christ's Crucifixion". *Tyndale Bulletin,* 43.2 (1992) 331–351.
http://www.skepticsquestions.com/wp-content/uploads/datingthecrucifixion.pdf.

Humphreys, J. *In God we Doubt: Confessions of a Failed Atheist.* London: Hodder and Stoughton, 2007.

International Standard Bible Encyclopedia, "Essenes".
https://www.internationalstandardbible.com/E/essenes.html

Irenaeus, Saint – of Lyons. *Adversus Haereses, Liber I.* Translated by Alexander Roberts and William Rambaut.
http://www.newadvent.org/fathers/0103126.htm

Jacobus, H.R. "The Zodiac Sign Names in the Dead Sea Scrolls (4q318): Features and Questions". *Aram,* 24 (2012) 311–31.

file:///c:/users/user/downloads/the_zodiac_sign_names_in_the_dead_sea_sc.pdf

Jewish Encyclopedia. "Nazarenes". In *Jewish Encyclopedia,* 1906/2021 https://www.jewishencyclopedia.com/articles/11393-nazarenes#anchor1

Josephus, Flavius. *The Wars of the Jews, or History of the Destruction of Jerusalem*. In *The Genuine Works of Flavius Josephus the Jewish Historian. Translated from the Original Greek, According to Havercamp's Accurate Edition*. Translated by William Whiston, 1737.
http://penelope.uchicago.edu/josephus/ant-18.html

----. *The Wars of the Jews, or History of the Destruction of Jerusalem*. Translated by W Whiston. Project Gutenberg E-Book, 2009.
https://www.gutenberg.org/files/2850/2850-h/2850-h.htm#link6noteref-20

Kaye, E.M. and J. Herskowitz. "Transient Post-Traumatic Cortical Blindness: Brief v Prolonged Syndromes in Childhood. *Journal Of Child Neurology*, 1986 Jul: 1(3): 206–10.
http://www.ncbi.nlm.nih.gov/pubmed/3598126

Keyser, J. "Drug Trade Thrived in Biblical Times". *Cannabis News*. 7 August 2002.
http://cannabisnews.com/news/13/thread13663.shtml

Kinzig, Wolfram, "The Nazoreans". In Oskar Skarsaune and Reidar Hvalvik, Eds., *Jewish Believers in Jesus*, Peabod, MS, Hendrickson, 2007, 463–87.

Kohler, K. "Ebionites". In *Jewish Encyclopedia*, 1906/2021.
http://www.jewishencyclopedia.com/articles/5411-ebionites

----. "Essenes." In *Jewish Encyclopedia*, 1906/2021
https://www.jewishencyclopedia.com/articles/5867-essenes#anchor24

Kolb, B. and I.Q. Wishaw. *Fundamentals of Human Neuropsychology*. New York: Worth, 2009.

König, Adrio. *Die Groot Geloofswoordeboek*. Vereeniging: Christelike Uitgewersmaatskappy. 2006.

Korsness et al. "An fMRI Study of Auditory Hallucinations in Patients with Epilepsy". *Epilepsia*, 51(4): 610–17.

http://onlinelibrary.wiley.com/doi/10.1111/j.1528-1167.2009.02338.x/pdf

Lamar, C.D. et al. "Post-Traumatic Epilepsy: Review of Risks, Pathophysiology, and Potential Biomarkers". *Journal of Neuropsychiatry and Clinical Neuroscience.* 26.2, Spring 2014. http://www.ncbi.nlm.nih.gov/pubmed/24763802

Landsborough, D. "St Paul and Temporal Lobe Epilepsy". *Journal of Neurology, Neurosurgery and Psychiatry* 1987: 50: 659–664. http://www.ncbi.nlm.nih.gov/pmc/articles/pmc1032067/pdf/jnnpsy00553-0001.pdf

Lezak, M.D. et al. *Neuropsychological Assessment.* New York: Oxford University Press, 2012.

Ludemann, G. *Heretics: The Other Side of Early Christianity.* Atlanta: John Knox, 1996.

Luschnig, C.E. and L.J. Luschnig. "The Teaching of the Twelve Apostles: A Greek Reader with Introduction and Notes." http://www.worldwidegreek.com/downloads/didache.pdf

Mack, B.L. *The Lost Gospel: The Book of Q & Christian Origins.* Shaftesbury: Element, 1994.

Magee, Michael D. "Christianity Revealed: Seeking the Historical Jesus". AskWhy! Publications, Frome, UK, 2003. file:///C:/Users/User/Downloads/Seeking_the_Historical_Jesus%20(3).pdf

Magiorkinis, E. et al. "Hallmarks in the History of Epilepsy: From Antiquity till the Twentieth Century". *Ancient History encyclopedia, 2012.* http://www.ancient.eu/article/394/#

Malina, Bruce J.: *On the Genre and Message of Revelation: Star Visions and Sky Journeys*, Peabody, MS, 1995.

Mason, Steve, "Josephus on the Essenes". *Biblical Archaeology Society Staff,* May 26, 2021. https://www.biblicalarchaeology.org/daily/biblical-artifacts/dead-sea-scrolls/josephus-on-the-essenes/

Mcallister, T.W. and R.B. Ferrell. "Evaluation and Treatment of Psychosis after Traumatic Brain Injury." *Neurorehabilitation.* 17 (2002) 357–368.

BIBLIOGRAPHY

http://iospress.metapress,com/content/j7kx3b4tqq7dapqe/
McClintock and Strong Biblical Cyclopedia, "Jessaeans".
https://www.biblicalcyclopedia.com/J/jessaeans.html

Metcalf, E. and P.F. Bass, P.F. "Head Injuries can Lead to Serious Vision Problems". *Everyday Health Media, 2009.*
http://www.everydayhealth.com/vision-center/head-injuries.aspx

Meyers, E.M. and M.A. Chancey. *Alexander to Constantine: Archaeology of the Land of the Bible.* New Haven: Yale University Press, 2012.

Nasrai, Abba Yesai. "Cherubic Sword: A Qabbalistic Glossary (With Some Nazorean Terms)".
https://www.faculty.umb.edu/gary_zabel/Courses/Phil%2081b/Philosophy%20of%20Magic/Arcana/Kabbalah/glossary9.htm

NASA. "Eclipse Web Site: Catalog of Solar Eclipses, 0001 To 100 Ce – 0029 Nov 24".
https://eclipse.gsfc.nasa.gov/5mcsemap/0001-0100/29-11-24.gif

---. "Eclipse Web Site: Catalog Of Lunar Eclipses, 0001 To 100 Ce – 0029 Dec 09."
https://eclipse.gsfc.nasa.gov/5mclemap/0001-0100/le0029-12-09p.gif

---. "Eclipse Predictions: Lunar Eclipses from 0001 to 0100, Jerusalem, Israel."
http://eclipse.gsfc.nasa.gov/jlex/jlex-as.html

Ngo, R. "Judaea Capta Coin Uncovered in Bethsaida Excavations". *Biblical Archaeology*, 09.07.2016.
http://www.biblicalarchaeology.org/daily/ancient-cultures/ancient-israel/judaea-capta-coin-uncovered-in-bethsaida-excavations/

Nicholl, J. "Neuropsychiatric Sequelae of Traumatic Brain Injury". *Semin Neurol* 2009; 29(3): 247–55.
http://medscape.com/viewarticle/706300_1

Nyu Langone Comprehensive Epilepsy Center. "Occipital Lobe Epilepsy".
http://epilepsy.med.nyu.edu/epilepsy/types-epilepsy/occipital-lobe-epilepsy#sthash.h3sfumzv.dpbs

Oakes, L. and L. Gahlin. *Ancient Egypt: An Illustrated Reference to the Myths, Religions, Pyramids and Temples of the Land of the Pharaohs.* London: Hermes, 2004.

O'Callaghan, T. "Oliver Sacks Wants to Destigmatize Hallucinations". *New Scientist, Nov 11 2012.* Nicholl, 2009.

Ontario Consultants on Religious Tolerance. "The Virgin Birth (Conception) of Jesus".
http://www.religioustolerance.org/virgin_b1.htm

Origenes Adamnatios. *Contra Celsum.*
http://www.documentacatholicaomnia.eu/03d/0185-0254,_origenes,_contra_celsus,_en.pdf

Orlov, A. *The Atoning Dyad: The Two Goats of Yom Kippur in the Apocalypse of Abraham.* Studia Judaeoslavica, 8; Leiden: Brill, 2016.

Paine, Tom. *The Age of Reason.* London: Freethought Publishing Company, 1880. http://www.gutenberg.org/files/3743/3743-h/3743-h.htm

Painter, J. *Just James – The Brother of Jesus in History and Tradition.* Minneapolis: Fortress, 1999.

Pelikan, J.J. "Jesus Christ". In *Encyclopædia Britannica*, 2010.

Pixner, Bargil, "Jerusalem's Essene Gateway: Where the Community Lived in Jesus' Time". *Biblical Archaeological Review,* May/June 1997.
http://www.centuryone.org/essene.html

Pollard, J.R.T and A.H.W. Adkins. "Greek Religion". In *Encyclopædia Britannica*, 2010.

Poole, G.W. "Josephus, Flavius". In *Encyclopaedia Britannica*, 2010.

Ratzon, Eshbal. "The First Jewish Astronomers: Lunar Theory and Reconstruction of a Dead Sea Scroll". *Science in Context* 30(2), 113–139 (2017).

BIBLIOGRAPHY

file:///C:/Users/User/Downloads/first_jewish_astronomers_l unar_theory_and_reconstruction_of_a_dead_sea_scroll%20(1).pdf

Riggs A.J. and J.E. Riggs. "Epilepsy's Role in the Historical Differentiation of Religion, Magic and Science". *Epilepsia,* March, 2005, Vol 46(3): 452–53 (Abstract).
http://onlinelibrary.wiley.com/doi/10.1111/j.0013-9580.2005.55405.x/full

Rylaarsdam, J. Coert et al. "Biblical Literature". In *Encyclopædia Britannica,* 2010.

Sacks, Oliver. *Hallucinations.* London: Picador, 2012.

———. *The River of Consciousness.* London: Picador, 2017.

Sanders, E.P. "Paul, the Apostle, Saint". In *Encyclopædia Britannica,* 2010.

Scholtz, Adelbert. *The Prophecies of Revelation: A Reconstruction of the Visions of John of Patmos.* Mauritius: Lambert Academic, 2017.

Sela, Shlomo, "Saturn and the Jews". In *Blog of the Katz Center for Advanced Judaic Studies, University of Pennsylvania,* November 10, 2017.
https://katz.sas.upenn.edu/resources/blog/saturn-and-jews

Serapion, Mara Bar. "Letter to his Son". In *Ante-Nicene Fathers,* Vol. 8. Edited by Alexander Roberts, James Donaldson, and A. Cleveland. Coxe Buffalo, NY: Christian Literature, 1886. Translated by B.P. Pratten. Revised and edited for New Advent by Kevin Knight.
http://www.newadvent.org/fathers/0863.htm

Shermer, M. *The Believing Brain: From Ghosts and Gods and Conspiracies – How we Construct Beliefs and Reinforce them as Truths.* New York: St Martin's, 2011.

Shurpin, Y. "Blood Moons, The Lunar Eclipse and The 15th of Av".
https://www.chabad.org/library/article_cdo/aid/4087075/jew ish/blood-moons-the-lunar-eclipse-and-the-15th-of-av.htm.

Spoor, T. "Concussion and Your Vision". *Sarasota Retina Institute,* 3 March 2013.

http://www.sarasotaretinainstitute.com/2013/03/concussion-and-your-vision-part-1/

Stein, D.L. "Psychedelics and the Ancient Near East. *Astor Blog.* 2010.

http://asorblog.org/psychedelics-and-the-ancient-near-east/

Stendahl, Krister and Emilie T. Sander, "Biblical Literature" In *Encyclopaedia Britannica,* 2010..

Stenger, Viktor J. *The New Atheism: Taking a Stand for Science and Reason.* New York: Prometheus, 2009.

Stephenson, F.R. "Eclipse". In *Encyclopaedia Britannica,* 2010.

Swaab, J. *Wij zijn ons Brein: Van Baarmoeder tot Alzheimer.* Amsterdam: Uitgeverij Contact. 2010.

Tabor, James, "Ebionites & Nazarenes: Tracking the Original Followers of Jesus". *Apocalypticism, December 29, 2015.*

https://jamestabor.com/ebionites-nazarenes-tracking-the-original-followers-of-jesus/

Thiede, C.P. and M. D'Ancona. *The Jesus Papyrus.* London: Phoenix, 1997.

Toy, C.H., "Psalms of Solomon, The." In *Jewish Encyclopedia.*

https://www.jewishencyclopedia.com/articles/12411-psalms-of-solomon-the.

University of Bonn. "Dragnet For Epilepsy Genes". *Science Newsline : Medicine,* January 23, 2015.

http://www.sciencenewsline.com/articles/2015012316090017.html

Wallis, G. "What do Hallucinations Tell us about the Brain? *Brain Metrics,* June 27 2013.

http://www.nature.com/scitable/blog/brain-metrics/what_do_hallucinations_tell_us

Webb, J. et al. "Auditory Hallucinations Associated with Headaches Following Traumatic Brain Injury. *Cns Spectr.* 2010: 15(8): 539–40.

http://www.cnsspectrums.com/aspx/articledetail.aspx?articleid=2789

West, L.J. "Hallucinations". In *Encyclopaedia Britannica,* 2010.

BIBLIOGRAPHY

Westminster Confession of Faith, The
https://epc.org/wp-content/uploads/files/1-who-we-are/b-about-the-epc/wcf-modernenglish.pdf

White, J. "Concussion, Traumatic Brain Injury and Seizures." http://mnepilepsy.org/news/concussion-traumatic-brain-injury-and-seizures/

Wilson, Barry. *How Jesus Became Christian: The Early Christians and the Transformation of a Jewish Teacher into the Son of God.* London: Phoenix, 2000.

Wolmarans, Hansie. "Jesus, die Heroïese Patroon, en Ons." In *Die Nuwe Hervorming,* edited by Piet Muller, 196–224. Pretoria: Protea, 2002.

Wright, N.T. "The Self-Revelation of God in Human History: A Dialogue on Jesus with N.T. Wright". In Antony Flew. *There is a God: How the World's most Notorious Atheist Changed his Mind.* New York: Harper Collins, 2007.

Young, R.C. "How Lunar and Solar Eclipses Shed Light on Biblical Events". *Bible And Spade,* 26.2 (2013). http://www.rcyoung.org/articles/eclipse1.pdf

Zillmer, E.A. *Principles of Neuropychology.* Belmont CA: Wadsworth, 2008.

BIBLIOGRAPHY

Picture Credits
Frontispiece
The 17th-Century Painting *Christ Crucified* By Diego Velázquez, Held By The Museo Del Prado In Madrid
https://www.pxfuel.com/en/search?q=inri

Solar Eclipses:
Downloaded From the Nasa Eclipse Web Site –
Https://Eclipse.Gsfc.Nasa.Gov/

Lunar Eclipses:
Downloaded From The Nasa Eclipse Web Site –
Https://Eclipse.Gsfc.Nasa.Gov/

Simulations of the Night Sky:
Downloaded from a computerized recreation of the night sky
http://www.stellarium.org/

Chapter 4
Map of Jerusalem
http://www.centuryone.org/essene.html

Iudea Capta Coin
https://www.vcoins.com/en/stores/sergey_nechayev_ancient_coins/200/product/vespasian_71ad_jewish_war_judaea_capta_superb_sestertius_ancient_roman_coin_rare/821939/default.aspx

Chapter 5:
Vespasian and Titus, the Roman generals and later emperors who vanquished the Jews during AD 66–70.
https://en.wikipedia.org/wiki/Vespasian
https://en.wikipedia.org/wiki/Titus

Chapter 6:
Caravaggio: Conversion of St Paul (1601)
http://studydroid.com/index.php?page=viewpack&packid=112798

www.ingramcontent.com/pod-product-compliance
Lightning Source LLC
Chambersburg PA
CBHW050817160426
43192CB00010B/1795